JEWISH
CHOICES,
JEWISH
VOICES

MONEY

D1416606

The Ben and Esther Rosenbloom Foundation
assisted in the publication of this book in honor
of Solomon Rosenbloom,
a man of great fortitude, wisdom, and justice.

JEWISH CHOICES, JEWISH VOICES

MONEY

EDITED BY
ELLIOT N. DORFF
AND
LOUIS E. NEWMAN

2008 • 5768
Philadelphia

The Jewish Publication Society
2100 Arch Street, 2nd floor
Philadelphia, PA 19103
www.jewishpub.org

Design and Composition by Progressive Information Technologies
Manufactured in the United States of America

08 09 10 11 12   10 9 8 7 6 5 4 3 2 1
ISBN: 978-0-8276-0861-0

Library of Congress Cataloging-in-Publication Data
Jewish choices, Jewish voices / edited by Elliot N. Dorff, Louis E. Newman. — 1st ed.
   v. cm.
   Includes bibliographical references and index.
   Contents: v. 1. The body
   ISBN 978-0-8276-0860-3 (BODY)
   ISBN 978-0-8276-0861-0 (MONEY)
   1. Jewish ethics.   2. Jews—Identity.   3. Body, Human—Religious aspects—
Judaism.   I. Dorff, Elliot N.   II. Newman, Louis E.

   BJ1285.2.J49 2008
   296.3'6—dc22   2007037402

JPS books are available at discounts for bulk purchases for reading groups, special sales and fundraising purchases. Custom editions, including personalized covers, can be created in larger quantities for special needs. For more information, please contact us at marketing@jewishpub.org or at this address: 2100 Arch Street, Philadelphia, PA 19103.

CONTENTS

Acknowledgments

No series of books such as this comes about without the creative energy and support of many individuals. We wish to thank, first and foremost, Ellen Frankel, editor-in-chief of The Jewish Publication Society, for her vision in first conceiving of this series, and her willingness to entrust it to our editorship. Her wise and patient guidance throughout the process of creating these volumes has been invaluable. The JPS National Council played a critical role early on as the scope and format of the series was in the development stage. Jane Shapiro's expertise as a Jewish educator was instrumental in helping us formulate the key issues around which to build each volume. Aaron Alexander and Steven Edelman-Blank, both rabbinical students at the University of Judaism (now the American Jewish University), collected, respectively, the traditional and the contemporary Jewish sources for this volume. We are indebted to them for their fine work in locating these materials. The staff of The Jewish Publication Society has been a pleasure to work with at every stage of the production process. We wish to thank especially Carol Hupping, Janet Liss, and Michael Pomante for their professionalism, their responsiveness to all our requests, their patience with all our delays, and their persistent good counsel. Finally, we wish to acknowledge Peter Wieben, a student at Carleton College, for all his work in assembling these volumes and preparing them for publication. His diligence and attention to detail are evident on every page of these books.

Description of the *Jewish Choices, Jewish Voices* Series

This series is intended to provide a forum for discussion of some of the most critical moral issues of our time. Because the Jewish tradition is rich in moral experience and insights, each volume includes Jewish materials from ancient, medieval, and modern sources. And because the Jewish tradition, from its very beginnings, is multivocal, the sources presented deliberately include diverse Jewish perspectives from the past. The process of Jewish wrestling with moral subjects, however, continues in our own day, not only theoretically but concretely and practically. And so each volume presents cases that raise difficult, modern moral issues, together with questions for reflection. We hope that these cases and questions will stimulate you to delve more deeply into the moral issues presented here.

We have also invited a number of modern Jews, representing a variety of backgrounds and Jewish perspectives, either to comment specifically on these cases or to reflect more generally on these moral problems as they come up in their own lives. These modern comments, a symposium of contemporary views and voices, bring new insights to the meaning and relevancy of the sources and take the conversation into new areas worth exploring.

In sum, then, the structure of each book is as follows:

Introduction: The topic of the book, the range of moral issues that it raises, and its import for modern life and for Judaism

I. **Case Studies and Jewish Sources:** Several cases illustrating some of the specific moral issues involved in this topic, including questions that highlight those issues, followed by ancient Jewish sources and an array of more modern writings relevant to those issues

II. **Symposium:** Contemporary perspectives by Jews on the cases or on the book's topic as they encounter it in their own lives

III. **Conclusion:** A summary of the underlying issues raised in the volume, together with some reflection on other related issues that may arise in the future

Seeing moral issues through a Jewish lens, even one that produces multiple refractions of the Jewish tradition and of Jewish modernity, will, we hope, enable modern Jews to grapple with those issues more intelligently and more sensitively. It is our deepest conviction that these voices from the Jewish tradition and today's Jewish community will invite you to consider your moral choices in a different light. At the very least, they give us all new questions and perspectives to ponder and, more often than not, moral wisdom and guidance.

Elliot N. Dorff
Louis E. Newman
July 2007

Introduction: Money

Rava said: When a person is led in for judgment [in the next world], God asks: "Did you transact your business honestly? Did you fix times for the study of the Torah? Did you fulfill your duty to establish a family?"

—*Babylonian Talmud Shabbat 31a*

T HE VERY first question that God asks each one of us after death, according to this passage in the Talmud, is whether we handled our monetary affairs honestly. The Talmud does not ask the expected questions—Did you murder anyone or injure anyone?—presumably because it assumes that most Jews do not do those things. What we are tempted to do, though, is to cheat in monetary affairs. Thus the way one handles one's money is a sensitive barometer of the moral mettle of a person and hence the very first question we are asked.

This book is about money—not how to get it but how to handle it morally. It describes how the Jewish tradition conceives of money, and it explores a number of moral issues that arise when the most scrupulous of us deal with money. The presumption of this book—and, indeed, of the Jewish tradition—is that most of us want to be moral. Even so, there are many times when we are not sure what the right thing to do is. This book does not always give firm answers to such questions—life is too complex for such certainty—but it certainly suggests guidelines. These guidelines come directly from Jewish sources themselves and from a number of modern Jews who have wrestled with such problems and have been asked to reflect on the best way to respond to them.

There clearly is a strong connection between money and work, for most of us make the money that sustains us through our work. Money, though, raises moral issues on its own, apart from the work that often produces it. This volume, the second in our series, will explore some of the problems and challenges inherent in how we perceive and handle money. Volume 3 will focus on some additional issues that we face in our work environments.

Fundamental Jewish Perspectives on Money

"Money is the root of all evil." Although often said, this does *not* bespeak a Jewish view—not unless we balance it with the equally exaggerated proposition that "money is the root of all good." Instead, like most things in life (food, sex, technology), money is morally neutral; it gains its moral valence on the basis of how it is used.

As with the body, the topic of Volume 1 in this series, though, American Jews are confronted by two very different perspectives about money in the American and Jewish traditions that they inherit. The Protestant ethic, which is at the core of much of America's attitude toward money, values not only work but the resources it produces, including money. Taken to its extreme, as it is all too often in modern America, money becomes the measure of a man—and now, increasingly, of a woman too. We speak of a person's "net worth," referring to how much money or other financial resources he or she has, as if that really defined the worth of a person.

Another source of American perspectives on money is the Enlightenment. In the Declaration of Independence, Thomas Jefferson said that it is a "self-evident truth" that all people are "endowed by their Creator with certain unalienable rights, that among these are life, liberty, and the pursuit of happiness." He borrowed that language from the 17th-century English philosopher John Locke; however, Locke had used the phrase "life, liberty, *and property*." According to Locke, we give up some of our rights in the state of nature in order to gain the benefits of civil society. Among these are our rights to all the monetary resources we have produced, and for every government to tax some portion of its citizens' income or assets. The burden of proof, however, rests with the government because it must prove not only that it requires this money but that it is using it fairly and wisely. Indeed, "no taxation without representation" was one of the primary battle cries that motivated Americans to revolt against England, and "taxation without representation" still appears on the license plates in Washington, D.C. as a protest against the inability of residents of the District to elect members to Congress. All monies and properties that I earn and that are not taken in taxes by the government, however, are mine to keep or spend in any legal way that I wish. The principle that I get to keep a significant part of what I earn is basic to capitalism, for that motivates me to earn at least as much as I need and maybe much, much more.

In sharp contrast, classical Jewish sources assert that by creating the world, God owns it all. As Moses says to the Israelites, "Mark, the heavens to their uttermost reaches belong to the Lord your God, the earth and all that is on it!" (Deuteronomy 10:14). Thus when I own something, I own it only vis-à-vis other human beings. Jewish law definitely does presume private ownership and not communalism; although communities may own property, individuals legally can and do own property as well. That ownership gives me the right to use my property in any way I please, except as restricted by law. Furthermore, my legal right to my property means that I can sue others in court if they damage my property or try to take it from me by force, and there the rule will be: "The one who wants to take something from his fellow bears the burden of proof [that it is rightfully his]" (Mishnah Bava Kamma 3:11; Bava Batra 9:6). All of this, however, applies only to my standing vis-à-vis other people and not vis-à-vis God.

Because God ultimately owns the whole earth, God can and does impose limits on my ownership. So, for example, according to Deuteronomy 22:8, I must put a parapet on my house's roof if it is flat and intended for people to use so that they do not fall off. Similarly, the Torah asserts that if I own land that I farm, I must leave to the poor the edges of the field and the crops that fall to the ground during harvest (Leviticus 19:9).

Furthermore, the community has both the moral right and the legal power in Jewish law to impose taxes, to require that individuals contribute to the communal fund and soup kitchen for the poor, and to regulate individuals' use of their property through such things as zoning rules. Ultimately, the communal court has the right to expropriate an individual's property, because "property that the court makes ownerless is ownerless (*hefker bet din hefker*)" (Tosefta, Shekalim 1:1; Babylonian Talmud, Yevamot 89b; Gittin 36b).

Moral Problems in the Use of Money

Although money is not in and of itself either bad or good, we can use it in both morally good and bad ways. Using money to sustain ourselves and our families and to provide for our own education and that of our children are obviously good uses of money, as is donating money to worthy causes. Spending money on vacations, entertainment, luxury items, and cosmetics, while not inherently good, is not necessarily bad either; the moral status of such spending depends on the degree to which one indulges oneself in such expenditures, in contrast to providing necessities for oneself, one's family, and others.

It is precisely this balance that is often hard for people to strike. Especially in America, which is so money driven, it is easy to fall prey to the assumption that money is God, that it is ultimately worthwhile. Some of this may result from the thin sense that Americans have of being part of a community. Americans glory in their individualism, an individualism that exceeds that of any other nation of the past or present. Individual freedoms bring many advantages, but their cost is that we lose a sense of community, of being there for each other. One clear example of this is our failure to date of providing health care for every American citizen. This lack of communally provided security leads some to focus on money as their only protection, for they cannot count on anyone else to supply what they need.

But the American idolization of money is not just a function of necessity because it extends to wealthy people as well. Americans, especially those professionals who earn big salaries and people in businesses that produce large profits, all too easily make money the center of their lives, the only thing that matters. Many of these people then engage in conspicuous consumption to show off how much money they have through the homes, clothes, jewelry, and cars they buy; the trips they take; and even the bar/bat mitzvah parties and weddings they plan. There is nothing wrong with having nice belongings; the issue is the degree to which that becomes the primary—and possibly the only—goal in life.

Another problem with money is the means that some people use to acquire it. Some engage in methods that are downright illegal—for example, cooking the books, violating securities laws, or cheating on income taxes. Others stay within the letter of the law but engage in ruthless business practices, beating the competition not with a superior product or service but with false advertising or with bargain prices in effect only as long as necessary to drive the competition out of business.

Then there are the issues in one's personal finances. To what extent do you have a responsibility to manage your finances well so that you can avoid bankruptcy and to whom do you have that duty—yourself, your family, the creditors on whom you will default, or the community as a whole? Further, what percentage of your income or resources should you give to charity? How should you make that decision in the first place? The cases created for this volume and the contributions written by a number of contemporary Jews from all walks of life and a range of Jewish affiliations address these and a number of other moral questions that money poses.

Applying the Tradition to Modern Problems

The Jewish sources in this volume substantiate what most readers of this volume probably assume—namely, that the Jewish tradition has much to say about how we conceive of money in the first place and how we earn and use it. As with everything else, however, some contemporary realities require that we apply Jewish concepts and values about money in new ways. For example, our ancestors could never have imagined our global economy run by the Internet, and they certainly did not deal with the new threats to honesty and privacy that the Internet raises in both its form and scope. Furthermore, they knew nothing about corporations. Indeed, contemporary corporate international issues are vastly more complicated than the ones raised by the agrarian and mercantile contexts that the Torah and later the Rabbis of the Mishnah and Talmud assume.

Many of the moral issues moderns face with money today, however, are identical to the ones Jews have confronted for generations, if not millennia, especially on a personal level. So, for example, the Torah already knows about the temptation to use dishonest weights and measures and prohibits us from giving in to that temptation (Leviticus 19:35–36; Deuteronomy 25:12–16); that precedent could easily be applied to new kinds of fraud. Similarly, the Torah is well aware of the fact that people will need loans, and it demands that we respond to that need in a way that does not make the debtors slaves for life (Exodus 22:24–26; Leviticus 25:25–55; Deuteronomy 24:10–13). Although we no longer press into slavery those debtors who cannot pay their debts, we can learn from the values articulated in these passages that the way we handle loans should be realistic and humane so that people do not lose their livelihoods, their homes, and their self-respect in taking out a loan. The Torah also knows that some people will be too poor to take out a loan, and it demands that we give food and money to the poor (Leviticus 19:9–10, 25:35–38; Deuteronomy 14:28–29, 15:7–11). The Torah also knows about the haughtiness and, indeed, the idolatry involved in presuming that I deserve full credit for everything I have, that "My own power and the might of my own hand have won this wealth for me" (Deuteronomy 8:17). Instead we should have the humility to recognize that others have played a role in affording us what we have, including, especially God: "Remember that it is the Lord your God who gives you the power to get wealth" (Deuteronomy 8:18). In these general ways, and in some very specific ways, much of what the Jewish tradition has to say about the moral issues surrounding money rings true and offers us wise counsel still today.

Historical Considerations

Jews as well as non-Jews commonly think of Jews as rich, and that is not a delusion: Jews are, in fact, one of the wealthiest segments of the American population. This, however, is a very new phenomenon. During most of Jewish history through the first half of the 20th century, Jewish communities were predominantly poor, and even today to think of Jews as uniformly well off is a distortion.

Historically, Jews were generally poor. That, in fact, is what makes the long Jewish history of helping the poor such a remarkable one, for in most cases it was the poor helping the absolutely destitute. Because of their poverty, Jews could not spare their children from helping the family earn a living for very long. Thus girls got no formal Jewish education whatsoever, and the one that boys got was short lived. The part of the opening number of *Fiddler on the Roof* that is sung by the boys is historically accurate: "At three I started Hebrew school; at ten I learned a trade." Thus when Jewish sources speak of money, one must understand that they are largely coming from a context in which most Jews had very little. There were exceptions, of course—Dona Gracia, who helped many refugees from Spain and Portugal emigrate to Turkey; Hayyim Solomon, who helped finance the American Revolutionary War; and the Rothschilds, who are still a family of very successful bankers all come immediately to mind—but they were the exceptions to the rule.

Even today, the economic condition of Jews is not uniformly comfortable. Studies, such as the recent research on the Jewish community of Los Angeles, show that as many as 20 percent of Jews live below the poverty line. Even those who are well off often find it hard to pay for Jewish services like day schools, summer camps, and synagogue membership, to say nothing of contributing to Jewish causes.

Still, although the economic and noneconomic manifestations of anti-Semitism are still significant in Europe, Jews in the United States and Canada now are treated as full citizens, with most, if not all, of the economic and social restrictions that plagued them until as late as the 1950s gone. In that environment, quite a number of Jews have found themselves in well-paying professions or businesses. Many are involved in major financial decisions of governmental bodies and large corporations.

Many Jews in their 20s and 30s are in the process of getting the education to join such professions or businesses or are already involved in them. As a result, the issues to which this book is devoted are very much part of the daily lives of Jewish young adults. We hope that the insights offered in this book from a plethora of Jewish sources and perspectives will aid its readers in working out at least some of the moral dilemmas of how to live morally with money.

PART I

⌘

CASE STUDIES AND JEWISH SOURCES

First Case Study: Morally Troubling Jobs

E LLEN AND Frank are two unrelated, single people in their 20s who are thinking about their future careers. Both come from middle-class families, and both still have college debts to pay off. Both of them have recently been offered jobs with salaries they never imagined that they could get at their age, Ellen in the clothing industry and Frank for a tobacco producer. Ellen discovers, however, that the firm offering her the job manufactures its clothing in factories in Southeast Asia where workers are exploited, receive low pay, and work under unsanitary and dangerous conditions. The tobacco producer offering Frank his job, in contrast, pays its workers well and even offers them substantial fringe benefits of health care and pensions; however, Frank has to confront the fact that this firm produces cancer-causing cigarettes and aggressively markets them to adolescents. The jobs offered to Ellen and Frank carry not only substantial salaries and fringe benefits but also offer them good opportunities for advancement and do not require more than 50 hours a week of work. Both Ellen and Frank are attracted by the possibility of paying off their debts and using their new, high-paying positions to help support their aging parents and even to make some significant contributions to charitable causes, but they are troubled by what they view as the moral compromises that they would have to make in working for such firms.

Questions

1. How should Ellen and Frank balance the personal benefits to them of these high-paying positions against the moral considerations that weigh against taking them?

2. Would your assessment of their choice differ if they came from wealthy families and therefore had no previous debts and did not really need to make a big salary?

3. Would your assessment change if they were married and had children for whom they wanted to establish funds for their future education?

4. Would your assessment change if they had no particular interest in charitable giving but had a strong penchant for expensive cars and trips to Europe?

5. Is the situation for Ellen different from that of Frank because of the moral issues involved in the two firms?

6. If Ellen is planning to get married and have a family and wants to earn a lot now in anticipation of time off that she expects to take from her career in the future to raise her children, does that change your assessment of what she should do now? If Frank also plans to marry (but not Ellen!) and have a family, does that affect what he should do now? If you answered differently for Ellen than for Frank, why?

Traditional Jewish Sources Relevant to All Cases

1. Genesis 1:27–28

And God created man in his image, in the image of God he created him, male and female He created them. God blessed them and God said to them, "Be fertile and increase, fill the earth and master it; rule the fish of the sea, the birds of the sky, and all the living things that creep on the earth."

2. Genesis 3:22

And the Lord God said, "Now that man has become like one of us, knowing good and bad."—[After Eve eats from the tree of knowledge of good and evil.]

3. Genesis 18:20–25

Then the Lord said, "The outrage of Sodom and Gomorrah is so great and their sin so grave! I will go down to see whether they have acted altogether according to the outcry that has reached Me; if not, I will take note." The men went on from there to Sodom, while Abraham remained standing before the Lord. Abraham came forward and said, "Will you sweep away the innocent along with the guilty? What if there should be fifty innocent within the city; will you then wipe out the place and not forgive it for the sake of the innocent fifty who are in it? Far be it from you to do such a thing, to bring death upon the innocent as well as the guilty, so that the innocent and the guilty fare alike. Far be it from you! Shall not the Judge of the earth deal justly?"

4. Leviticus 19:18

You shall not take vengeance or bear a grudge against your countrymen. Love your fellow as yourself: I am the LORD.

5. Leviticus 25:14

When you sell property to your neighbor, or buy property from your neighbor, you shall not wrong one another.

6. Deuteronomy 25:13–16

You shall not have in your pouch alternative weights, larger and smaller. You shall not have in your house alternative measures, a larger and a smaller. You must have completely honest weights and completely honest measures, if you are to endure long on the soil that the Lord your God is giving you. For everyone who does those things, everyone who deals dishonestly, is abhorrent to the Lord your God.

7. Micah 6:8

He has told you, O man, what is good,
And what does the Lord require of you?
Only to do justice
And to love goodness,
And to walk modestly with your God;
Then will your name achieve wisdom.

8. Isaiah 1:17

Learn to do good.
Devote yourselves to justice;
Aid the wronged.
Uphold the rights of the orphan;
Defend the cause of the widow.

9. Mishnah, Avot, Ethics of the Fathers 1:14

This was another favorite teaching of his (Hillel):
If I am not for me, who will be?
If I am not for myself alone, what am I?
And if not now, when?

10. Mishnah, Avot, Ethics of the Fathers 2:1

Rabbi (Judah the Prince) taught:
What is the path of virtue that a person should follow?
That which brings honor to one's maker as well as respect from one's fellow human beings. . . .

Weigh the loss incurred in performing a commandment against the gain; conversely, weigh the gain of a sin against the loss.

Ponder three things and you will avoid committing a sin.
Keep in mind what is above you:
An Eye that sees, an Ear that hears,
A Book in which all your deeds are recorded.

11. Mishnah, Avot, Ethics of the Fathers 1:7

Nitai, of Arbel, taught:
Keep far from an evil neighbor;
Be not a partner with an evil person;
Never despair of retribution for the wicked.

12. Mishnah, Avot, Ethics of the Fathers 4:1

Who is mighty? Those who conquer their evil impulse; as it is written: "One who is slow to anger is better than the mighty, and one who rules over his spirit [is better] than the one who conquers his city" (Proverbs 16:32).

Who is rich? Those who are content with their portion; as it is written: "When you eat the labor of your hands, happy will you be and all will be well with you" (Psalms 128:2).

13. Mishnah, Avot, Ethics of the Fathers 4:17

There are three crowns: The crown of Torah, the crown of Priesthood, and the crown of Royalty. The crown of a good name surpasses them all.

14. Bereshit Rabbah 9:7

If it were not for the evil [that is, the self-regarding] impulse, no person would build a house, or marry, or procreate, or engage in business.

15. Maimonides, Mishneh Torah, Laws of Sales 10:1

It is forbidden to cheat people in trade, or to deceive them. This rule applies to both Jew and non-Jew. One who knows there is a deficiency in his products is obligated to notify the buyer.

16. Babylonian Talmud, Shabbat 31a

Rava said: When one is brought [after death] for judgment, they ask: "Have you done business in good faith? Did you make time for study? Did you [engage] in procreation? Did you yearn for salvation? Did you delve deeply into wisdom? Did you discern one matter from another?" In any case: "Reverence for the Lord—that was his treasure" (Isaiah, 33:6).

Traditional Jewish Sources

On Sweatshops

1. Babylonian Talmud, Nedarim 49b

Rabbi Yehudah used to go into the House of Study [the academy] carrying a pitcher on his shoulders. He would say, "Great is work, as it gives honor to the worker." Rabbi Shimon would carry a basket on his shoulders, and would say, "Great is work, as it gives honor to the worker."

2. Exodus Rabbah 1:27

[The slavery the Egyptians imposed on the Israelites was made especially burdensome because they placed] a heavy burden on a child and a light burden on an adult; a man's burden on a woman and a woman's burden on a man; the burden of an elderly person on a youth, and the burden of a youth on an elderly person.

3. Leviticus 19:13

Do not oppress your neighbor and do not rob him. Do not keep the wages of the worker with you until morning.

4. Deuteronomy 24:14–15

Do not oppress the hired laborer who is poor and needy, whether he is one of your people or one of the sojourners in your land within your gates. Give him his wages in the daytime, and do not let the sun set on them, for he is poor, and his life depends on them, lest he cry out to God about you, for this will be counted as a sin for you.

5. Babylonian Talmud, Bava Metzi'a 112a

"His life depends on them" (Deuteronomy 24:15). Why does he climb a ladder or hang from a tree or risk death? Is it not for his wages? Another interpretation—"His life depends on them" indicates that anyone who denies a hired laborer his wages, it is as though he takes his life from him.

6. Mishnah, Bava Metzi'a 7:1

One who hires workers and instructs them to begin work early and to stay late—in a place in which it is not the custom to begin work early and to stay late, the employer may not force them to do so. In a place in which it is the custom to feed the workers, he must do so. In a place in which it is the custom to distribute sweets, he must do so. Everything goes according to the custom of the land.

There was an incident concerning Rabbi Yochanan ben Matya, who told his son, "Go, hire us workers." His son went and promised them food [without specifying what kind, or how much]. When he returned, his father said to him, "My son! Even if you gave them a feast like that of King Solomon, you would not have fulfilled your obligation toward them, for they are the children of Abraham, Isaac, and Jacob. However, as they have not yet begun to work, go back and say to them that their employment is conditional on their not demanding more than bread and vegetables." Rabbi Shimon ben Gamliel said, "It is not necessary to make such a stipulation. Everything goes according to the custom of the place."

7. Babylonian Talmud, Bava Metzi'a 83a

We need [the example given in source 6—the editors] for the case in which the employer raises the workers' wages. In the case in which he says to them, "I raised your wages in order that you would begin work early and stay late," they may reply, "You raised our wages in order that we would do better work."

8. Mishnah, Bava Metzi'a 4:12

A shopkeeper must not give children parched corn or nuts, for he entices them to buy everything in his place [which amounts to unfair competition]. The Sages permit this. R. Judah forbids lowering prices for the same reason, but the Sages permit it.

On Working for Tobacco Companies

9. Babylonian Talmud, Kiddushin 82b

We are taught on early rabbinic authority: There is no occupation that lacks usefulness. Fortunate is the one whose parents are engaged in worthy pursuits; woe to the one whose parents are engaged in dishonorable pursuits.

10. Babylonian Talmud, Hullin 10a

Regulations concerning danger to life are more imperative than ritual prohibitions.

11. Shulhan Arukh, Yoreh De'ah 116:5 (Rama)

One should distance oneself from things that may lead to danger, for a danger to life is more serious than a [ritual] prohibition, and one should be more worried about a possible danger to life than a possible [transgression] of a prohibition. Therefore, the Sages prohibited one to walk in a place of danger, such as close to a leaning or shaky wall [it may fall] or alone at night. They also prohibited drinking water from streams at night or placing one's mouth on a flowing pipe of water to drink. For these things may lead to danger. . . .

All of these things are intended to avoid danger, and one who is concerned with his health will avoid them. And it is prohibited to rely on a saving miracle, or to endanger oneself in a like way.

12. Exodus 21:22–25

When men fight . . . if injury ensues, the penalty shall be life for life, eye for eye, tooth for tooth, hand for hand, foot for foot, burn for burn, wound for wound, bruise for bruise.

13. Mishnah, Bava Kamma 8:1

One who injures a person is liable [to pay the victim] on five counts: for the injuries, for pain, for healing, for loss of time, and for insult.

14. Babylonian Talmud, Sukkah 29b

Rabbi Yohanan said in the name of Rabbi Simeon ben Yohai [on the matter of why a stolen *lulav* is not valid for use on Sukkot]:

It is [invalid] because [it is a case of] a commandment being performed through a sin.

15. Babylonian Talmud, Kiddushin 42b

. . . it is an established principle that an agent cannot be appointed to perform a violation of the law [and thus everyone is responsible for his or her own violations].

16. Babylonian Talmud, Hullin 94a

We are taught on early rabbinic authority that a person should not sell anyone shoes made from the hide of an animal that died by itself and claim the animal was actually slaughtered, for two reasons: First, because the seller is deceiving the buyer. Second, there is an element of danger involved [for the animal may have died from a disease that could endanger the buyer of the shoes].

17. Maimonides, Mishneh Torah, Laws of Murder and Protection of Life 12:14

Everything that is forbidden to sell to an idolater similarly may not be sold to an Israelite who is a thief, since in doing so one strengthens the hand of transgressors and places an obstacle before them. And so too anyone who places an obstacle before the blind by offering advice that is not appropriate, or by strengthening the hands of transgressors who are blind and cannot see the true path on account of an inner failing (*ta'ut libo*) thereby violates a negative commandment, as it is written, "you shall not place a stumbling-block before the blind" (Leviticus 19:14).

Contemporary Sources

Source 1

The more deeply immersed I became in the thinking of the prophets, the more powerfully it became clear to me what the lives of the prophets sought to convey: that morally speaking there is no limit to the concern one must feel for the suffering of human beings. It also became clear to me that in regard to cruelties committed in the name of a free society, some are guilty, while all are responsible.

Abraham Joshua Heschel, "The Reasons for My Involvement in the Peace Movement," in *Moral Grandeur and Spiritual Audacity: Essays,* edited by Susannah Heschel (New York: Farrar, Straus, Giroux, 1996), 225.

Source 2

Exploitation of workers, heedless polluting, the economic abandonment of communities, manipulative advertising, and other everyday features of the corporate world represent transgressions of Jewish law, which places many controls on economic enterprise in the name of the community's well-being. Management decision-making based not on a "stakeholder" philosophy but on the narrowest definition of "the bottom line" is unacceptable. As the Talmud slyly puts it: "There is the story of a man who was clearing stones out of his domain and throwing them into the public domain. A pious man, seeing him, said to him, 'Wretch, why do you remove stones from a domain that is yours to a domain that is not yours?'"

Lawrence Bush and Jeffrey Dekro, "Judaism and Corporations," *Tikkun* 15, no. 2 (March/April 2000): 32.

Source 3

The Rabbis taught that certain occupations that disturbed the moral balance of the world would not bring prosperity. To modern ears it is not clear if they expected such occupations to bring down specific Divine or demonic interventions, or were warning of the intrinsic, systemic consequences of bad action. Perhaps to their own ears such a distinction was meaningless; perhaps to them "Divine intervention" and "systematic consequences" were the same.

Arthur Waskow, *Down to Earth Judaism: Food, Money, Sex, and the Rest of Life* (New York: William Morrow, 1995), 170.

Source 4

"Face the damn facts, Henry," Hammond said irritably. "This isn't America. This isn't even Costa Rica. This is my island. I own it. And nothing is going to stop me from opening Jurassic Park to all the children of the world." He chuckled. "Or, at least, to the rich ones. And I tell you, they'll love it."

Michael Chrichton, *Jurassic Park* (New York: Ballantine Books, 1990), 203.

Source 5

If I were a Brazilian without land or money or the means to feed my children, I would be burning the rain forest too.

Sting [Gordon Matthew Sumner], quoted in *The Columbia Dictionary of Quotations* (New York: Columbia University Press, 1993), 283.

Source 6

Somehow, Doris Houston was holding it all together. The Champaign (Ill.) researcher in drug addiction was working full-time and completing a PhD at the University of Illinois. At the same time, she was caring for her teenage son. Then, starting about 2½ years ago, she noticed that her widowed, 84-year-old mother, Anna, who lived in Chicago, was having memory problems. Houston first arranged for family members to stay with her mom. Then Anna suffered a stroke. Although her mother did not want to leave Chicago, Houston felt she had no choice but to bring her to Champaign. Her mother lives with her now, and Houston is juggling parenting, a full-time job, and her role as caregiver. Today more than 30 million Americans are caring for an elderly parent, according to a study by the AARP and the National Alliance for Caregiving. As the nation ages, elder care is rapidly becoming the biggest family issue facing workers and their employers. According to one study, the value of this unpaid care exceeds $257 billion annually. Caring for aging parents is a responsibility none of us relishes. It can create emotional and financial hardship. You will almost certainly have to take time off from work, and the pressures of elder care can compromise your relationships with spouses, partners, and children. You will also tumble headlong into a world filled with such jargon as activities of daily living, skilled nursing facilities, and Medicaid spend-downs.

> Howard Gleckman, "When a Parent Needs Help; How to Pull Together an Elder Care Plan That Makes Sense For You, Your Siblings—And Your Parents," *Business Week*, July 12, 2004, 89.

Second Case Study: Credit Card Debt

Jennifer recently graduated from college and began her first job as an administrative assistant at a publishing house. When Jennifer first came to college, several credit card companies actively pursued her and persuaded her to open accounts with them. During the course of her four years in college, Jennifer accumulated considerable debts on these cards, and now receives regular and increasingly threatening letters and calls from the companies. On her salary, she cannot afford to pay off her debts, which are growing rapidly because of high interest charges and penalty fees. Jennifer blames the credit card companies for her predicament, pointing to their predatory promotion on college campuses, their exorbitant interest rates, and their excessive profits. She figures that they will lose track of her now that she's moved to another city and will eventually give up harassing her for payment. However, she worries that she now has a bad credit rating and will be unable to get a mortgage or buy a car on credit in the future.

Questions

1. Is Jennifer justified in refusing to pay for her credit card debt? Was she taken advantage of by these companies?

2. Would it make any difference in your assessment if you knew that Jennifer suffers from bipolar illness and that she racked up most of her debt during her manic phases? Do credit card companies have an obligation to withhold credit cards from those incapable of managing their money responsibly?

3. If Jennifer were your friend and confided in you about her predicament, would you advise her to pay her debts, even if that meant depriving herself of the few luxuries she can now afford on her modest salary? If she refused, would you lend her the money? Would you call the companies yourself and give them her new address?

Traditional Sources

(*Note:* For traditional Jewish sources relevant to all cases, see pp. 3–6.)

1. Babylonian Talmud, Pesachim 22b

Whence do we learn that one does not hand a cup of wine to a Nazarite [who has taken a vow to abstain from alcohol] and the limb from a live animal to a gentile [who is bound by the Noahide law, which forbids eating such meat]? Scripture teaches, "You shall not place a stumbling-block before the blind" (Leviticus 19:14).

2. Maimonides, Mishneh Torah, Laws of Lending and Borrowing 2:7

It is forbidden for anyone to lend money [to another] without witnesses. Even lending to a Sage (*talmid hakham*) [without witnesses] is forbidden, unless one lends on security. And it is still better if the loan is recorded in a document.

Anyone who lends money without witnesses violates "You shall not place a stumbling-block before the blind" (Leviticus 19:14) and brings a curse upon himself.

3. Mishnah, Avot, Ethics of the Fathers 2:9 (2:14 in some editions)

Rabbi Yohanan said: Look about you and tell me, which is the way in life that one should avoid?

Rabbi Eliezer said: a begrudging eye.

Rabbi Joshua said: an evil colleague.

Rabbi Yose said: an evil neighbor.

Rabbi Shimon said: one who borrows and does not repay, for borrowing from a person is like borrowing from God, as the Bible says, "The wicked borrows and does not repay, but the righteous one [here understood to mean God] deals graciously and gives" (Psalms 37:21).

Rabbi Elazar said: a begrudging heart.

Rabbi Yohanan said to them: I prefer the answer of Rabbi Elazar ben Arakh, for his view includes all of yours.

4. Maimonides, Mishneh Torah, Laws of Lending and Borrowing 1:2–3

2. Anyone who presses a poor person [to pay back a loan], knowing that he [the poor person] has nothing with which to pay him back violates a negative commandment, for the Torah says, "Do not act toward him [a poor person] as a creditor" [Exodus 22:24]. . . .

3. It is forbidden for a person to appear before someone indebted to him when he [the creditor] knows that he [the debtor] has nothing. Even to pass by him [is forbidden] so as not to frighten him or embarrass him, even though he [the creditor] is not claiming his money back and all the more so if he is [trying to collect the loan]. And just as it is forbidden for this one [the creditor] to claim [the loan when he knows the debtor cannot pay him], so it is forbidden for that one [the debtor] to keep the money of his friend in his hand and say to him, "Go and come back [another day]" when he has the money [to pay him back], as the Bible says, "Do not say to your fellow, 'Come back again; I'll give it to you tomorrow' when you have it with you" (Proverbs 3:28). It is similarly forbidden for the borrower to take a loan and spend it for unnecessary things and to waste it such that the creditor will never be able to collect it, even if the creditor is very rich; one who does this is an evil person, as it says, "The wicked person borrows and does not repay" (Psalms 37:21). The Sages commanded, "Let your friend's money be as dear to you as your own" (Ethics of the Fathers 2:12 [2:17 in some editions]).

5. Babylonian Talmud, Pesachim 118a

R. Joshua ben Levi said: "When the first person heard what God said to him, 'But your food shall be the grass of the field' (Genesis 3:18), he cried and said [to God]: 'Lord of the world, shall I and my cattle eat in a single stall?' But when he [Adam] heard Him say to him: 'By the sweat of your brow shall you get to eat bread . . .' (Genesis 3:19), his [Adam's] mind was eased."

6. Maimonides, Mishneh Torah, Laws of Stealing and Loss 1:9–12

9. Anyone who covets someone else's male or female slave or house or utensils or anything else that it is possible for him to buy from him and he talked at length about it among his friends and implored him until he bought it from him, even if he gave him much money, he has violated a negative commandment, as the Torah says, "Do not covet" (Exodus 20:14). We do not flog a person for violating this prohibition because it does not include an act. He does not violate this prohibition until he purchases the item that he craved, as it says, "you shall not covet the silver and gold on them [images of other gods] and keep it for yourselves" (Deuteronomy 7:25), [the latter phrase indicating] that it must be coveting that includes an action [to be culpable for lashes].

10. If A desires B's house or B's wife or B's goods or any similar thing that A might buy from B, A transgresses a negative commandment as soon as he thinks in his heart how he might acquire the desired object and allows his mind to be seduced by it. For Scripture says, 'You shall not desire . . . " (Deuteronomy 5:18), and desire is in one's heart alone [in contrast to coveting, which is accompanied by an action].

11. Desiring leads to coveting, and coveting leads to stealing, for if the owners did not want to sell [the object], even though he offered much money and talked about it endlessly among his friends, he will ultimately steal it, as it says, "They covet fields and seize them, houses and take them away" (Micah 2:2). And if the owners stood against him to save their property or prevented him from stealing it, he will ultimately kill [to get it]. Go and learn from the case of Ahab and [the vineyard of] Neboth [I Kings 21].

12. Thus you have learned that one who desires [other people's things] violates one prohibition; one who buys something that he desires through pestering the owners or through pleading with them violates two

prohibitions. Therefore the Torah says [both] "Do not desire" and "Do not covet." And if he stole [the object], he violates three prohibitions.

Contemporary Sources

Source 1

To steal from a brother or sister is evil. To *not* steal from the institutions that are the pillars of the Pig Empire is equally immoral.

Abbie Hoffman, *Steal This Book* (New York: Four Doors Eight Windows, 1996), iv.

Source 2

If you are not in debt of some kind, you're unusual. For most Americans today, debt is a part of daily life. Using a credit card, borrowing for college, applying for a mortgage to buy a house—taking on debts such as these may well be the first experience many of us have with a financial institution. All the more reason to understand and master the dos and don'ts of debt. Until you know how to manage debt, it's almost impossible to save, invest, or build an intimate financial relationship with a life partner based on anything resembling a strong foundation. Until your debt is in control and part of your life plan, you will not achieve financial freedom.

Suze Orman, *The Road to Wealth: A Comprehensive Guide to Your Money: Everything You Need to Know in Good and Bad Times* (New York: Riverhead Books 2001), 3.

Source 3

People go into debt for many reasons, but I have often noticed a correlation—an inverse relationship—between self-esteem and bad debt. I call the result your "debt set point." The lower your self-esteem, the higher your debt set point. If you generally feel good about yourself and are living in a responsible way, chances are you don't have a lot of debt on your balance sheet. If you are spending more money than you have, you are probably spending money not only to obtain more goods and services but also to acquire more self-esteem. The less self-esteem you have, the more debt you create.

Suze Orman, *The Road to Wealth: A Comprehensive Guide to Your Money: Everything You Need to Know in Good and Bad Times* (New York: Riverhead Books 2001), 4.

Source 4

Pops: Hey, how're you guys fixin' to pay?

Kermit: What are our choices?

Pops: A: Credit card; B: Cash; C: Sneak out in the middle of the night.

Fozzie: We'll take C.

Pops: Very popular choice.

"Happiness Hotel," *The Great Muppet Caper* [DVD] directed by Jim Henson (Burbank, Calif.: Walt Disney Home Entertainment, 2005).

Source 5

Marius had never given up for a single day. He had undergone everything, in the shape of privation; he had done everything, except get into debt. He gave himself this credit that he had never owed a sow to anybody. For him a debt was the beginning of slavery. He felt even that a creditor is worse than a master; for a master owns only your person, a creditor owns your dignity and can belabor that.

Victor Hugo, *Les Misérables*, translated by Charles E. Wilbour (New York: Everyman's Library/Alfred A. Knopf, Inc., 1997), 674.

Source 6

Speak as you think, be what you are, pay your debts of all kinds. I prefer to be known as sound and solvent, and my word as good as my bond, and to be what cannot be skipped, or dissipated, or undermined, to all the éclat in the universe. This reality is the foundation of friendship, religion, poetry, and art.

Ralph Waldo Emerson, quoted in *The Columbia World of Quotations* (New York: Columbia University Press, 1996), www.bartleby.com/66/61/20261.html (accessed December 2, 2007).

Source 7

It's rather grisly, isn't it, how soon a living man becomes nothing more than a collection of stocks and bonds and debts and real estate?

John Dos Passos quoted in *The Columbia World of Quotations* (New York: Columbia University Press, 1996), www.bartleby.com/66/62/17562.html (accessed December 2, 2007).

Third Case Study: Child Care

Ira and Jackie have been married for five years and now have a three-year-old and a one-year-old. They both work full-time and therefore need to make arrangements for the care of their children during the day. They have two choices, both of which raise moral questions. They could put their children in a large day-care facility, where they know the staff is underpaid and turns over frequently. They have concerns about the quality of the care their children will get as well as qualms about exploitative working conditions that they would be aiding and abetting. On the other hand, if they were to hire a nanny, they could not pay Social Security or any benefits, and they feel that is a problem, both legally and morally.

Questions

1. Where should Ira and Jackie place/enroll their children?

2. Should one of them instead resign from his or her job to take care of the children even if this means that they will be financially strapped now and will have no money to put away for the future education of their children?

3. Should one of them consider taking a position in another company that offers childcare to its employees but pays less well and offers much less professional satisfaction?

Traditional Sources

(*Note:* For traditional Jewish sources relevant to all cases, see p. 3.)

On Having and Educating Children
1. Babylonian Talmud, Yevamot 64a

Another early rabbinic teaching: R. Eliezer said, "Anyone who does not engage in procreation is as though one sheds blood; For it is written, 'whoever sheds the blood of man . . . ' (Genesis, 9:6) And the next verse states, 'Be fertile, then, and increase, abound on the earth and increase on it'" (Genesis 9:7). R. Yaakov said: "It is as if one diminished the Divine Image, as it is written, '. . . . For in his image did God make man.' (Genesis, 9:6) And the next verse states, 'Be fertile, then, and increase, abound on the earth and increase on it'" (Genesis 9:7).

18

2. Maimonides, Mishneh Torah, Laws of Behavior 5:11

The way of a sensible person is to establish for himself an occupation by which to support himself, then buy a house, and afterwards get married . . .

3. Deuteronomy 6:4–9

Hear, O Israel! The Lord is God, the Lord alone. You shall love the Lord your God with all your heart and with all your soul and with all your might. Take to heart these instructions with which I charge you this day. Impress them upon your children. Recite them when you stay at home and when you are away, when you lie down and when you get up. Bind them as a sign on your hand and let them serve as a symbol on your forehead. Inscribe them on the doorposts of your home and on your gates.

4. Rashi to Deuteronomy 6:5

With all your might: With all your property. There are people whose property is more important to them than their bodies. Therefore [the text explicitly] states [that one should love God] *with all of your might* [that is, with all of your property].

5. Babylonian Talmud, Kiddushin 29a

Our Rabbis taught: A man is responsible to circumcise his son, to redeem him [from the Temple service if he is the first born, "*pidyon ha-ben*"], to teach him Torah, to marry him off to a woman, and to teach him a trade, and there are those who say he must also teach him to swim. Rabbi Judah says: "Anyone who fails to teach his son a trade teaches him to steal."

6. Otzar Dinim U'minhagim, "Av v'Am," 1

We have learned from tradition that the Mother is also responsible for the education of her children, as it is said: "My son, heed the discipline of your father, and do not forsake the instruction of your mother" (Proverbs 1:8).

7. Babylonian Talmud, Bava Batra 21a

Rav Judah said in the name of Rav: Rabbi Joshua ben Gamla should be remembered for good, for had it not been for him the Torah would have been forgotten in Israel. For at first, the boy who had a father was taught Torah by him, while the boy who had no father did not learn. Later, they appointed teachers of boys in Jerusalem, and the boys who had fathers were brought by them [to the teachers] and were taught; those who had no fathers were still not brought. So then they ordered that the teachers should be appointed in every district, and they brought to them lads of the age of sixteen or seventeen. And when the teacher was cross with any of the lads, the lads would kick at him and run away. So then Rabbi Joshua ben Gamla ordered that teachers should be appointed in every district and in every city and the boys should be sent to them at the age of six or seven years.

On the Dignity of Work

8. Babylonian Talmud, Nedarim 49b

When Rabbi Judah went to the schoolhouse, he would carry a pitcher of water on his shoulder and say: "Work is great, for it honors those who do it."

9. Babylonian Talmud, Kiddushin 82b

We are taught on early rabbinic authority: There is no occupation that does not have its usefulness. Fortunate is the one whose parents are engaged in worthy pursuits; woe to the one whose parents are engaged in dishonorable pursuits.

10. Babylonian Talmud, Pesachim 118a

R. Joshua ben Levi said: "When the first person heard what God said to him: 'But your food shall be the grass of the field' (Genesis 3:18), he cried and said [to God]: 'Lord of the world, shall I and my cattle eat in a single stall?' But when he [Adam] heard Him say to him: 'By the sweat of your brow shall you get to eat bread . . . ' (Genesis 3:19), his [Adam's] mind was eased."

11. A. Cohen, Everyman's Talmud (New York: Dutton, 1949), 194

We read of a few of them [the classical rabbis] belonging to wealthy families, but the majority were humble workmen who earned a precarious livelihood. The story of Hillel's poverty has already been told [B. *Yoma* 35b]. Of other Rabbis we learn that Akiba used to collect a bundle of wood daily and exist on the price he received for it [*Avot d'Rabbi Natan* 6]; Joshua was a charcoal-burner and lived in a room the walls of which were begrimed by his manner of work (B. *Berahkot* 28a); Meir was a scribe (B. *Eruvin* 13a); Yose bar Halafta was a worker in leather (B. *Shabbat* 49b); Yohanan was a maker of sandals (M. *Avot* 4:14); Judah was a baker (J. *Haggigah* 77b); and Abba Saul held a menial position as a kneader of dough (B. *Peshahim* 34a), while he mentions that he had also been a grave-digger (B. *Niddah* 24b).

12. Babylonian Talmud, Berachot 17a

A favorite saying of the Rabbis of [the academy] at Yavneh was this: I am a creature of God, and my uneducated neighbor is also God's creature. My work is in the city, and his work is in the field. I rise early for my work, and he rises early for his. Just as he cannot excel in my work, so I cannot excel in his. Will you say that I do great things [in the way of Torah] and he does little? We have learned [B. *Menahot* 110a] that it matters not whether one does much or little as long as he directs his heart to Heaven.

On Fairness to Workers
13. Mishnah, Bava Metzi'a 7:1

If someone hired workers and told them to come early or to stay late, in a place where the custom is not to come early or stay late, he is not permitted to force them to do so. In a place where the custom is to feed [workers], he must feed them. [In a place where the custom is to give them] dessert, he must give them dessert—everything goes according to local custom.

14. Babylonian Talmud, Bava Metzi'a 112a

Whoever withholds a worker's wages, it is as if he takes his life from him.

15. Babylonian Talmud, Sukkah 29b

Rav said: The property of householders can be confiscated [by the government] for four things: (1) Because they withheld wages of a hired hand, (2) because they oppressed a hired hand, (3) because they took the yoke off of their necks and placed it on their fellow's neck, (4) and because they were arrogant. But arrogance outweighs the others. And about humble people it is written: "But the lowly [humble] shall inherit the land and delight in abundant well-being" (Psalms 37:11).

16. Babylonian Talmud, Sukkah 45b

A father should be careful to draw his son away from falsehood.

17. Maimonides, Mishneh Torah, Laws of Sales 10:1

It is forbidden to cheat people in trade, or to deceive them. This rule applies to both Jew and non-Jew.

18. Maimonides, Mishneh Torah, Laws of Murder and Protection of Life 12:14

Everything that is forbidden to sell to an idolater similarly may not be sold to an Israelite who is a thief, since in doing so one strengthens the hand of transgressors and places an obstacle before them. And so too anyone who places an obstacle before the blind by offering advice that is not appropriate, or by strengthening the hands of transgressors who are blind and cannot see the true path on account of an inner failing (*ta'ut libo*) thereby violates a negative commandment, as it is written, "you shall not place a stumbling-block before the blind." (Leviticus 19:14)

Contemporary Sources

Source 1

I am Rabbi David Saperstein, Director of the Religious Action Center of Reform Judaism. At the recent convention of our parent organization, the Union of American Hebrew Congregations, 4000 delegates overwhelmingly passed a resolution supporting living wage campaigns. We did this because for more than 3000 years our tradition, our teachings and our values have instructed us to provide fair and timely wages to the laborer.

> David Saperstein, "Statement of Rabbi David Saperstein, Director, Religious Action Center of Reform Judaism on the Need for a Living Wage," avaliable at rac.org/Articles/index.cfm?id=443&pge_prg_id=4368 (accessed June 25, 2006).

Source 2

In any case, if we leave aside Perry and a few other high-quality, high-cost programs, and force ourselves to look at day care as it is rather than as we might wish it to be, the facts are as implacable as their explanation seems obvious. The typical child in day care simply does not receive the same amount of individual attention, or the same degree of focused intensity, he would receive from a parent. There is rarely the same degree of continuity in the relationship between child and adult. Nor is there a family history or sense of lineage to help a child establish his identity. As for the people running the programs, caring for children is, for many of them, not a source of pride or prestige; they just go through the motions.

In short, the best and the most natural domicile for raising a child is the family. Obviously. It is only because we have made ourselves so fearful of claiming that *any* human arrangement is "natural" that it becomes necessary to search through data and argument to establish what is, obviously, so. That—and the fact that a substantial body of opinion holds otherwise.

Joseph Adelson, "What We Know about Day Care." *Commentary* 104, no. 5, (November 1997): 53.

Source 3

Consider President Clinton's failed appointment of Zöe Baird in the first few days of his new Administration. Baird was removed from consideration after it was revealed that she had hired an undocumented worker as her child's nanny. How is it possible that Zöe Baird, who earned half a million dollars a year, couldn't find the money to pay for legal child care?

The defense offered by Clinton Administration was that otherwise her record was blameless. Other than her crime, which she knowingly committed and hired a lawyer to defend, she was strictly within the law. Let's leave aside that men in government are never asked how they got their child care, how could a woman who cares passionately for the right thing, and is infused with a passion for social justice, not care about oppressing someone who is here without papers by paying her too little to be able to save retirement money?

In our secularized culture we have made justice and goodness mutually exclusive. An authority on the big picture—the equality of human beings, the liberation of the world, freedom from hunger and want and poverty—doesn't have time to say "thank you." Too many of those concerned with individual acts of kindness and beauty think that politics are pointless, that all politicians are necessarily corrupt, and mendacity is the way of the world. So long as we sever righteousness and leadership, we remain powerless to transform the world.

Bradley Shavit Artson, "Personal Ethics and Social Justice," *Jewish Spectator* (spring 1999): 44.

Source 4

But whatever keeps wages low—and I'm sure my comments have barely scratched the surface—the result is that many people earn far less than they need to live on. How much is that? The Economic Policy Institute recently reviewed dozens of studies of what constitutes a "living wage" and came up with an average figure of $30,000 a year for a family of one adult and two children, which amounts to a wage of $14 an hour. This is not the very minimum such a family could live on; the budget includes health insurance, a telephone, and child care at a licensed center, for example, which are well beyond the reach of millions. But it does not include restaurant meals, video rentals, Internet access, wine and liquor, cigarettes and lottery tickets, or even very much meat. The shocking thing is that the majority of American workers, about 60 percent, earn less than $14 an hour. Many of them get by by teaming up with another wage earner, a spouse or grown child. Some draw on government help in the form of food stamps, housing vouchers, the earned income tax credit, or—for those coming off welfare in relatively generous states—subsidized child care. But others—single mothers for example—have nothing but their own wages to live on, no matter how many mouths there are to feed.

Employers will look at the $30,000 figure, which is over twice what they currently pay entry-level workers, and see nothing but bankruptcy ahead. Indeed, it is probably impossible for the private sector to provide everyone with an adequate standard of living through wages, or even wages plus benefits, alone: too much of what we need, such as reliable child care, is just too expensive, even for middle-class families. Most civilized nations compensate for the inadequacy of wages by providing relatively generous public services such as health insurance, free or subsidized child care, subsidized housing, and effective public transportation. But the United States, for all its wealth, leaves its citizens to fend for themselves— facing market-based rents, for example, on their wages alone. For millions of Americans, that $10—or even $8 or $6—hourly wage is all there is.

Barbara Ehrenreich. *Nickel and Dimed: On (Not) Getting by in America* (New York: Metropolitan/Owl, 2001), 213–214.

Source 5

No slogan of democracy, no battle cry of freedom, is more striving than the American parent's simple statement, which all of you have heard many times: "I want my child to go to college."

Lyndon Baines Johnson, quoted in *The Columbia World of Quotations* (New York: Columbia University Press, 1996), www.bartleby.com/66/13/ 31113.html (accessed December 2, 2007).

Fourth Case Study: Allocating Public Money

You are a state legislator. Your state, like many others, has recently required substantial budget cuts in order to remain fiscally sound. Even if taxes were raised significantly, there simply would be no way to avoid either cutting programs or reducing the amount of money allocated to them. You are committed to voting in a way that is consistent with your understanding of Jewish values. Assuming that there is no emergency in any of the following social programs but that there is a continuing need for them. Assume that the current allotments are as follows:

a. Transportation (including repairing olds roads and bridges and building new ones, as well as public transportation) = $2.5 billion

b. K–12 education (including teachers' salaries, maintaining and constructing school buildings, administrative costs, and free lunch programs for the poor) = $8.25 billion

c. Higher education (state college and university system) = $1.3 billion

d. Health and human services (including retraining programs for the unemployed, senior services, services for the disabled, mental health services, and drug and alcohol abuse prevention programs) = $6.5 billion

e. Law enforcement (including police, fire, prisons, and terrorist prevention measures) = $900 million

f. Government (including salaries for legislators, state employees, and their aids; cars and office expenses; and communications costs) = $550 million

g. Parks and recreation (including state parks and wildlife refuges and water conservation programs) = $100 million

Questions

1. How would you prioritize the current social programs?
2. Assume $2 billion must be cut from the state budget; how would you achieve this?

Traditional Sources

(*Note:* For traditional Jewish sources relevant to all cases, see p. 3.)

1. Leviticus 25:35–38

If your kinsman, being in straits, comes under your authority, and you hold him as though a resident alien, let him live by your side. Do not take interest or profit from him, but fear your God. Let him live by your side as kinsman. Do not lend him money at advance interest, or give him your food at accrued interest. I the LORD am your God, who brought you out of the land of Egypt, to give you the land of Canaan, to be your God.

2. Micah 6:8

"He has told you, O man, what is good,
And what does the Lord require of you?
Only to do justice
And to love goodness,
And to walk modestly with your God."

3. Mishnah, Megillah 4:1

If the townspeople sell the town square [where at times religious ceremonies were performed], they may buy with the proceeds a synagogue [on the principle that we may exchange something for a more holy purpose but not for a less holy one]; if they sell a synagogue, they may buy with the proceeds an ark [in which to place scrolls of the Torah]; if they sell an ark, they may buy wrappings [for the Torah scrolls]; if they sell wrappings, they may buy scrolls [of the biblical books other than the Pentateuch]; if they sell [such] scrolls, they may buy a scroll of the Torah. But if they sell a scroll of the Torah, they may not buy with the proceeds scrolls [of the other biblical books]; if they sell scrolls [of the other biblical books], they may not buy wrappings [for the Torah scroll]; if they sell wrappings [for the Torah scroll], they may not buy an ark; if they sell an ark, they may not buy a synagogue; and if they sell a synagogue, they may not buy a town square. The same applies to any money left over [from any of these purchases].

4. Mishnah, Sanhedrin 4:5

For this reason Adam was created alone: to teach you that destroying a single life is to destroy a whole world, even as to save a whole life is to save a whole world. And for the sake of the peace of creation, that no one should say to another, "My ancestor was greater than yours." And so that heretics cannot say, "There are many powers in heaven." And to proclaim the greatness of the Holy Blessed One, for when a person makes many coins with one die, they all look alike, but the Holy One stamps every human being with the die of the first Adam, and none resembles the other. For this reason, each and every person must declare, "For my sake the world was created."

5. Mishnah, Avot, Ethics of the Fathers 2:8

Another favorite teaching of his (Hillel):
More flesh, more worms; more possessions, more worries. . . .
However—more Torah, more life; more study with colleagues, more wisdom; more council, more understanding; more good deeds, more peace.

6. Mishnah, Avot, Ethics of the Fathers 2:17

Rabbi Yose taught:
The property of others should be as precious to you as your own. . . .
Let all of your deeds be for the sake of heaven.

7. Mishnah, Avot, Ethics of the Fathers 3:13

This was another favorite teaching of his (Rabbi Hanina ben Dosa):
When one pleases one's fellow creatures, God is pleased;
When one does not please one's fellow creatures, God is not pleased.

8. Mishnah, Avot, Ethics of the Fathers 4:1

. . . Who is honored? Those who honor all people; as it is written: "Those who honor Me, I will honor; but those who scorn Me will be despised" (1 Samuel 2:30).

9. Mishnah, Avot, Ethics of the Fathers 4:9

Rabbi Yishmael, his (Rabbi Yose's) son, taught:
A person who shuns the office of judge avoids enmity, theft, and perjury; but one who treats the judicial process lightly is a fool, wicked and arrogant.

10. Tanna d'bei Eliyahu Zuta 1

Whosoever is able to perform an act of charity and does not, to save a person and does not, causes himself to perish.

11. Pesikta Rabbati, Chapter 22, The Ten Commandments, "Lo Tissa"

One who accepts upon oneself a position of political authority for benefit is considered an adulterer . . .

12. Babylonian Talmud, Pesachim 87b

Rabbi Yohanan said: Woe to those who have great authority, for it buries those who possess it.

13. Babylonian Talmud, *Sotah* 14a

Rabbi Hama, son of Rabbi Hanina, said: "What is the meaning of the verse, 'You shall walk behind the Lord your God'? (Deuteronomy 13:5) . . . [It means that] a person should imitate the righteous ways of the Holy One, blessed be God. Just as the Lord clothed the naked . . . so too you must supply clothes to the naked [poor]. Just as the Holy Blessed One visited the sick . . . so too you should visit the sick. Just as the Holy Blessed One buried the dead . . . so too you must bury the dead. Just as the Holy Blessed One comforted mourners . . . so too you should comfort mourners."

14. Babylonian Talmud, Gittin 61a

We do not prevent poor non-Jews from collecting produce under the Laws of Gleaning, the Forgotten Sheaf, and the Corner of the Field— for the sake of keeping peace.

Our Rabbis taught: We support the non-Jewish poor with the Jewish poor, and we visit the non-Jewish sick with the Jewish sick, and we bury the non-Jewish dead with the Jewish dead—for the sake of keeping peace.

15. Maimonides, Mishneh Torah, Laws of Gifts to the Poor 7:7

The Jewish and non-Jewish poor must be cared for in order to keep the peace.

16. Babylonian Talmud, Sanhedrin 17b

And it has been taught on early rabbinic authority: A scholar should not reside in a city where [any] of the following ten things is missing: (1) A court of justice that can impose flagellation and monetary penalties; (2) a charity fund, collected by two people and distributed by three [to ensure honesty and wise policies of distribution]; (3) a synagogue; (4) public baths; (5) toilet facilities; (6) a circumciser (*mohel*); (7) a surgeon; (8) a notary [for writing official documents]; (9) a slaughterer (*shohet*); (10) a schoolmaster. Rabbi Akiva is quoted [as including] also several kinds of fruit [in the list] because they are beneficial for eyesight.

17. Maimonides, Mishneh Torah, Laws of Gifts to the Poor 10:7

The highest merit in giving charity is attained by the person who comes to the aid of another in bad circumstances before he reaches the stage of actual poverty. Such aid may be in the form of a substantial gift presented in an honorable manner, or a loan, or the forming of a partnership with him for the transaction of some business enterprise, or assistance in obtaining some employment for him, so that he will not be forced to seek charity from his fellow men. Concerning this Scripture says, "You shall strengthen him (Leviticus 25:35)," that is, you shall assist him so that he does not fall.

18. Shulchan Arukh, Orach Chayyim 153:2

However, to do the opposite [of the order in Source 3 above] i.e., [to use the sale money] to acquire something with a lesser amount of holiness is forbidden. Even if they used some of the money to buy something with a higher degree of holiness, they may not [buy something] with the remainder of the money that has a lesser degree of holiness.

19. Shulchan Arukh, Orach Chayyim 153:6

They may sell a synagogue or other holy articles—even a Torah scroll, in order to support students or help marry off an orphan with the money.

20. Shulchan Arukh, Yoreh De'ah 249:16

There are those who say that the commandment to [build and support] a synagogue takes precedence over the commandment to give charity to the poor, but the commandment to give money to the youth to learn Torah or to the sick among the poor takes precedence over the commandment to build and support a synagogue.

21. Shulchan Arukh, Yoreh De'ah 251:7–8

One must feed the hungry before one clothes the naked [since starvation is taken to be a more direct threat to a person's life than exposure]. If a man and a woman came to ask for food, we put the woman before the man [because the man can beg with less danger to himself]; similarly, if a man and a woman came to ask for clothing, and similarly, if a male orphan and a female orphan came to ask for funds to be married, we put the woman before the man.

22. Babylonian Talmud, Ta'anit 23a

One day he [Honi] was journeying on the road and he saw a man planting a carob tree; he asked him, "How long does it take [for this tree] to bear fruit?" The man replied: "Seventy years." He then asked him: "Are you certain that you will live another seventy years?" The man replied: "I found [matured] carob trees in the world; as my ancestors planted these for me, so I too plant these for my children."

Contemporary Sources

Source 1

To sum up: Whereas the liberal believes that to every problem there is a solution, and the radical believes that to any problem there is only the general answer of wholesale transformation, I believe that we can have only partial and less than wholly satisfying answers to the social problems in question. Whereas the liberal believes that social policies make steady progress in nibbling away at the agenda of problems set by the forces of industrialization and urbanization, and whereas the radical believes that social policy has made only insignificant inroads into these problems, I believe that social policy has ameliorated the problems we have inherited but that it has also given rise to other problems no less grave in their effect on human happiness than those which have been successfully modified.

The liberal has a solution, and the radical has a solution. Do I have a solution? I began this discussion by saying that the breakdown of traditional modes of behavior is the chief cause of our social problems. That, of course, is another way of saying industrialism and urbanization, but I put it in the terms I did because I am increasingly convinced that some important part of the solution to our social problems lies in traditional practices and traditional restraints. Since the past is not recoverable, what guidance could this possibly give? It gives two forms of guidance: first it counsels hesitation in the development of social policies that sanction the abandonment of traditional practices, and second, and perhaps more helpful, it suggests that the creation and building of new traditions must be taken more seriously as a requirement of social policy itself.

Nathan Glazer, "The Limits of Social Policy," *Commentary* 52, no. 3 (September 1971): 54.

Source 2

In other critical areas of social policy, too, the breakdown of traditional measures, traditional restraints, traditional organization, represents, if not the major factor in the crisis, a significant contribution to it. Even in an area apparently so far removed from tradition as health and medical care, the weakening of traditional forms or organization can be found upon examination to be playing a substantial role, as when we discover that drug addiction is now the chief cause of death—and who knows what other frightful consequences—among young men in New York.

Ultimately, we are not kept healthy, I believe, by new scientific knowledge or more effective cures or even better-organized medical-care services. We are kept healthy by certain patterns of life. These, it is true, are modified for the better by increased scientific knowledge, but this knowledge is itself communicated through such functioning traditional organizations as the school, the voluntary organization, the family. We are kept healthy by having access to traditional means of support in distress and illness, through the family, the neighborhood, the informal social organization. We are kept healthy by decent care in organization where certain traditionally-oriented occupations (like nursing and the maintenance of cleanliness) still manage to perform their functions. I will not argue the case for the significance of traditional patterns in maintaining health at length here; but I believe it is a persuasive one.

Nathan Glazer, "The Limits of Social Policy," *Commentary* 52, no. 3 (September 1971): 57.

Source 3

Like most Jewish liberals in recent years, I have been chastened in my hopes that government can produce greater social justice. People are not as moral or rational as I once believed; professors and journalists are not as smart; and government is not only as corruptible as other Americans institutions but has its own proclivities for producing evil with the good. Messianic liberalism has died, but practical and Jewish reasons keep me and many Jews from going conservative.

We fear the power interests behind the new conservatives. Ronald Reagan, having the Right, may now speak softly as he sidles toward the Center to avoid the Goldwater stigma. . . .

We believe a constitutional government is more to be trusted to improve society than is an open market, benign neglect, or other natural arrangements. . . .

Eugene B. Borowitz in Morris B. Abram et al., "Liberals and the Jews: A Symposium," *Commentary* 69, no. 1 (January 1980): 23.

Source 4

I believe government, organized authority, or the State is necessary *only* to maintain or protect property and monopoly. It has been proven efficient in that function only. As a promoter of individual liberty, human well-being and social harmony, which alone constitute real order, government stands condemned by all the great men of the world.

Emma Goldman, quoted in *Red Emma Speaks: An Emma Goldman Reader,* edited by Alix Kates Shulman, 3rd ed. (Atlantic Highlands, N.J.: Humanities Press International, 1996), 51.

Source 5

The more I try to imagine a Jewish outlook on money that may be useful to my grandchildren and the future beyond them, the more I find myself concerned about issues that do not at first glance seem to be about money: Will there be ozone and water, plankton and forests to share life with them? Will there be a lively Jewish community to share spiritual sustenance with them?

Then, close behind, come images that are about money—not if my own grandchildren will have enough money to live on (which is what my grandparents chiefly worried about), but if others around them will: How thick will be the crowds of the homeless, desperate people in their cities? Will their hospital emergency room be full of people who cannot afford to go anywhere else to get routine care? Will their government be spending ten times as much for prisons as for schools?

Arthur Waskow, *Down to Earth Judaism: Food, Money, Sex, and the Rest of Life* (New York: William Morrow, 1995), 212.

Source 6

Government does not solve problems; it subsidizes them.

Ronald Reagan, quoted in *The Columbia World of Quotations* (New York: Columbia University Press, 1996), www.bartleby.com/66/13/46113.html (accessed December 2, 2007).

Source 7

We might come closer to balancing the Budget if all of us lived closer to the Commandments and the Golden Rule.

Ronald Reagan, quoted in *The Columbia World of Quotations* (New York: Columbia University Press, 1996), www.bartleby.com/66/96/46096.html (accessed December 2, 2007).

Source 8

Government has no other end but the preservation of Property.

John Locke, quoted in *The Columbia World of Quotations* (New York: Columbia University Press, 1996), www.bartleby.com/66/20/36620.html (accessed December 2, 2007).

Source 9

Every society gets the kind of criminal it deserves. What is equally true is that every community gets the kind of law enforcement it insists on.

Robert F. Kennedy, quoted in *The Columbia World of Quotations* (New York: Columbia University Press, 1996), www.bartleby.com/66/59/32459.html (accessed December 2, 2007).

Source 10

[M]y conception of liberty does not permit an individual citizen or a group of citizens to commit acts of depredation against nature in such a way as to harm their neighbors and especially to harm the future generations of Americans. If many years ago we had had the necessary knowledge, and especially the necessary willingness on the part of the Federal Government, we would have saved a sum, a sum of money which has cost the taxpayers of America two billion dollars.

Franklin D. Roosevelt, [sound recording], *FDR Speaks* edited by Henry Steele Commager (Washington, D.C.: Washington Records, 1960).

Source 11

The nation that destroys its soil destroys itself.

Franklin D. Roosevelt, quoted in *The Columbia World of Quotations* (New York: Columbia University Press, 1996), www.bartleby.com/66/42/46942.html (accessed December 2, 2007).

Source 12

Because I wouldn't give you two cents for all your fancy rules if behind them they didn't have a little bit of plain, ordinary, everyday kindness and a—a little lookin' out for the other fella too.

"Democracy in Action," *Mr. Smith Goes to Washington* [DVD], directed by Frank Capra (Los Angeles: Columbia TriStar Home Video, 1999).

Source 13

Education costs money, but then so does ignorance.

Sir Claus Moser, quoted in *The Columbia Dictionary of Quotations,* ed. Robert Andrews (New York: Columbia University Press, 1993), 266.

PART II

❧

SYMPOSIUM

Money: Social Issues

Working for a Living? A Jewish Perspective on the Living Wage Movement

Jill Jacobs

I N THE mid-1990s, pastors in innercity Baltimore began to notice that working people constituted an alarmingly high percentage of their churches' soup kitchen, food pantry, and shelter clients. Indeed, statistical evidence corroborates the observations of these pastors. As of 2005, in America's 24 largest cities, 40 percent of adults who applied for emergency food assistance and 15 percent of homeless adults were employed. Sparked by the ministers' concern, a coalition of religious, labor, and community groups in Baltimore launched a campaign that succeeded in raising wages for some workers first to $6.10/hour and, as of June 2006, to $9.30/hour. This victory launched what would become a national "living wage" movement. Since 1994, more than 140 other cities and other jurisdictions have passed living wage laws, which mandate wage levels either for specific groups of employees—such as city employees, employees at businesses of a certain size, or those working for companies with government contracts—or for all workers in a particular area. The mandated living wage ranges from $6.75 (Albuquerque, New Mexico) to $13 plus health insurance or $14.75 without health insurance (Fairfax, California). Most of these laws mandate a process for increasing the wage level each year.

Support for living wage legislation seems to transcend political boundaries. In one remarkable illustration of this phenomenon, residents of Florida voted in 2004 to reelect George W. Bush *and* to raise the state's minimum wage. Although primarily identified with progressive community groups and scholars, the living wage movement has clearly touched a nerve for people on all sides of the political spectrum.

This essay examines the growth and effect of the living wage movement and considers some Jewish perspectives on this approach to alleviating poverty. It addresses questions such as: Why a living wage and why now? What is the economic effect of the living wage? How can Judaism's insight about the relationship between the employer and the employee and about wages and work conditions inform our opinion about the living wage campaigns? Should Jews pay a living wage and support related legislation?

Why a living wage? To understand the current living wage movement, we first should take a step back and consider the history of the

U.S. minimum wage. Even though the current federal minimum wage does not enable a family to live, the original intention of the minimum wage law was exactly the same as those who now push for living wage legislation—namely, to establish a wage floor that would eliminate gross exploitation of desperate workers and enable them to earn a living. Thus, despite the disparity between the import of the two terms today, they began with the same meaning and intention.

Congress instituted the minimum wage as part of the 1938 Fair Labor Standards Act. The text of this legislation describes the minimum wage as a necessary means of eliminating "labor conditions detrimental to the maintenance of the minimum standard of living necessary for health, efficiency, and general well-being of workers."[1] Though intended to guarantee a basic standard of living for all workers, this act failed to tie minimum wage levels to external factors, such as the consumer price index (according to which Social Security benefits, for instance, are adjusted). As of 2006, the federal minimum wage had not increased since 1997, and the purchasing power of the minimum wage had reached its lowest level since 1955.[2] A person who works 40 hours a week at the federal minimum wage of $5.15/hour will earn only $10,712/year—less than the 2004 federal poverty line of $14,776 for a family of three. This figure becomes even more disturbing when we consider the widespread critiques that point out that the official poverty line falls far below the real costs of food, housing, health care, child care, transportation, and other necessities.[3]

The living wage movement recognizes that minimum wage workers cannot actually afford their families' basic needs and thus, as the Baltimore pastors observed, often request help from emergency food and housing programs. In general, living wage campaigns attempt to secure a wage that is based either on the self-sufficiency index—a measure of the real costs of basic goods in a particular county—or on the cost of housing (which constitutes most families' single largest expense) or on a percentage (usually 80 percent) of the median income for the area. Political

1. Fair Labor Standards Act of 1938 §2(a).
2. Jared Bernstein and Isaac Shapiro, *Buying Power of Minimum Wage at 51 Year Low* (Washington, D.C.: Center on Budget and Policy Priorities and Economic Policy Institute, 2006).
3. See Constance F. Citro and Robert T. Michael, eds., *Measuring Poverty: A New Approach* (Washington, D.C.: National Academies Press, 1995). This study, commissioned by the federal government during the Clinton administration, proposed changes in the way in which poverty is measured in the United States; with the change in administration, however, these suggestions were never implemented.

realities sometimes dictate that the living wage passed in a particular jurisdiction will not actually cover the cost of living, but these living wages always represent an improvement over the federal or state minimum wage. In most cases, the living wage legislation includes a mechanism for raising wages each year.

At this point, we will turn our discussion to examining Jewish perspectives on low-wage work and to considering what Judaism might teach us about the living wage issue.

Jewish Perceptions of Work and Workers

Paradoxically, traditional Jewish texts portray manual labor simultaneously as dignified and as potentially exploitative. One ancient text, for example, extols the value of work, commenting, "A person should love work, and not hate work. Just as the Torah was given through the covenant, so too, work was given through the covenant, as it says 'For six days you shall labor and do all of your work, and the seventh day is a Sabbath to your God.'"[4] More recently, Chaim David Halevy, the 20th-century legal scholar and former Sephardic chief rabbi of Tel Aviv, commented, "In the Jewish worldview, work is sacred—it is building and creating and is a partnership with God in the work of creation."[5]

While some of the Rabbis of the Talmud appear to be independently wealthy, others are described as working to support themselves. One text describes Rabbi Yehudah and Rabbi Shimon, both of whom lived during the first two centuries of the Common Era, walking into the *beit midrash* (study house) carrying pitchers and baskets and declaring, "'Great is work, as it gives honor to the one who does it.'"[6]

Even while singing the praises of hard work, the early Rabbis never forgot that the central narrative of Jewish history centers on an oppressive work situation—namely, the years of slavery in Egypt. During that time, the Jewish people suffered from harsh labor, lack of autonomy, and abuse at the hands of taskmasters who treated their slaves as somewhat less than human.

With this memory of slavery never far from their minds, the Rabbis set out to create a system of employment law that guarantees the dignity and well-being of both workers and employers. While recognizing that low-

---

4. Avot de-Rabbi Natan, Nusach A, chap. 11.
5. Chaim David Halevy, *Teshuvot Aseh L'cha Rav*, (Tel Aviv: Hava'adah L'hotza'at Kitvei Ha-rav Ha-gaon Chaim David Halevy, 1975).
6. B. Nedarim 49b.

wage workers are often desperate enough to work in subpar conditions, the Rabbis instituted protections aimed at minimizing the employer's ability to take advantage of his or her workers. This value is best encapsulated by the rabbinic gloss on the biblical verse, "For the children of Israel are [God's] servants,"[7] which the Rabbis took to mean "and not servants to servants."[8] Based on this principle, the Rabbis established protections against workers effectively becoming the slaves of their employers. Thus, in most situations, workers are allowed to quit a job in the middle of the day, even if there is potential for some financial loss on the part of the employer. Along a similar vein, a person may not work in another person's household for more than three years, lest this position may take on the appearance of servitude.[9] With their acknowledgment that employees can, in some cases, become like slaves, the Rabbis anticipated the contemporary American situation, in which many low-wage workers become entirely dependent on the goodwill of their employers for health insurance, housing, and even immigration status.

Wages and Working Conditions in Jewish Law

The concept of *minhag ha-makom* (the custom of the land) dictates much of Jewish labor law. That is—each employer is legally bound to adhere to the employment conditions that have become standard in a particular city or country. According to one key talmudic text:

> One who hires workers and instructs them to begin work early and to stay late—in a place in which it is not the custom to begin work early and to stay late, the employer may not force them to do so. In a place in which it is the custom to feed the workers, he must do so. In a place in which it is the custom to distribute sweets, he must do so. Everything goes according to the custom of the land.

> A story [is told] about Rabbi Yochanan ben Matya, who told his son, "Go, hire us workers." His son went and promised them food (without specifying what kind, or how much). When he returned, his father said to him, "My son! Even if you gave them a feast like that of King Solomon, you would not have fulfilled your obligation toward them, for they are the children of Abraham, Isaac and Jacob. However, as they have not yet begun to work, go back and say to them that their

---

7. Leviticus 25:55.
8. Babylonian Talmud, Bava Kamma 117b.
9. Rema, comment on Shulchan Arukh, Hoshen Mishpat 333:3.

employment is conditional on their not demanding more than bread and vegetables." Rabbi Shimon ben Gamliel said, "It is not necessary to make such a stipulation. Everything goes according to the custom of the place."[10]

At face value, this text simply spells out the principle that all employment conditions, from wages to hours to perquisites (such as food), should conform to the "custom of the place." Based on this text, many writers on Judaism and economics have concluded that Jewish law supports a free market system in which each employer is bound only to the custom of the place, regardless of what that custom might be.

A few elements within this text, and within later Jewish law, complicate this conclusion. First, Rabbi Yochanan ben Matya's response to his son introduces the idea that workers should be treated with the dignity that we would accord to the most honored of guests. Whereas low-wage workers in our society are often treated as invisible or as less than human, Rabbi Yochanan ben Matya forces us to think of these workers as members of our own families.

The most famous biblical passage on labor law also reminds us of the humanity and economic desperation of low-wage workers:

> Do not oppress the hired laborer who is poor and needy, whether he is one of your people or one of the sojourners in your land within your gates. Give him his wages in the daytime, and do not let the sun set on them, for he is poor, and his life depends on them, lest he cry out to God about you, for this will be counted as a sin for you. (Deuteronomy 24:14–15)[11]

This passage places low-wage workers, like widows and orphans, in the category of people in need of special protection. The text acknowledges both the worker's reliance on wages, and the employer's power to cheat the worker of these wages. The biblical realization that workers often put their lives on the line for the sake of money is driven home by a talmudic text that comments, "Why does he climb a ladder or hang from a tree and risk death? Is it not for his wages?"[12] This observation has particular resonance in a time when the incidence of fatal work injuries is increasing each year in some industries (such as construction and agriculture)

---

10. Mishnah Bava Metzi'a 7:1.
11. Cf. Leviticus 19:13.
12. Babylonian Talmud Bava Metzi'a 112a.

and among some ethnic groups (such as Latinos, among whom the rate of fatal work injuries increased 28 percent from 1997 to 2004 on a per capita basis).[13] Workers desperate for money continue to risk their lives by working under unsafe conditions.

In a poignant comment on this biblical verse, Ramban (Rabbi Moshe ben Nahman, 1194–1270) explains:

> For he is poor, like the majority of hired laborers, and he depends on the wages to buy food by which to live. . . . If he does not collect the wages right away as he is leaving work, he will go home, and his wages will remain with you until the morning, and he will die of hunger that night.[14]

With this observation, Ramban reminds us that most low-wage workers live from payday to payday and depend on the prompt payment of wages in order to provide for their families' basic needs. Ramban places the responsibility for guaranteeing the worker's health firmly on the employer, who is most probably aware of his or her immense power in the life of the worker. An employer who fails to pay on time cannot try to reassign blame for any negative consequences in the life of the worker. What is surprising in Ramban's comment, though, is his assumption that a worker who *is* paid on time *will* be able to provide for the needs of his or her family. In our day, when the ranks of the working poor are growing steadily, we can no longer expect a low-wage worker's pay to provide sufficiently for the needs of his or her family.

Interfering with the Market

We now have established two potentially contradictory principles: On the one hand, working conditions (including wages) should conform to the "custom of the place"; on the other hand, the employer is obligated to ensure the basic well-being of the workers. In the United States, the "custom of the land" is a minimum wage of $5.15/hour but, as we have seen, this pay does not even suffice to lift a family above the poverty line. How, then, can we reconcile these two principles?

---

13. This observation has particular resonance in a time when the incidence of fatal work injuries is increasing each year in some industries (such as construction and agriculture) and when the incidence of fatalities resulting from falls increased 15% from 2005–2006. Workers desperate for money continue to risk their lives by working under unsafe conditions. See www.bls.gov/news.release/cfoi.nr0.htm.
14. Ramban comment to Deuteronomy 24:14 (author's own translation).

We may begin with the Rabbis' own willingness to interfere with market conditions. One early rabbinic text permits the "people of the city" to stipulate workers' wages as well as prices and measurements.[15] Later Jewish legal writings understand this text as also granting labor unions and other collections of workers permission to set wages for the entire group.[16] The Rabbis thus find a way around the strict reliance on custom to establish wages and other working conditions. When the free market does not produce wages on which a person can live, the community may interfere with the standard wage rates.

Within Jewish tradition, we have at least one example of the community imposing a living wage on communal workers. According to the medieval scholar Moses Maimonides (1138–1204), certain workers in the Temple (which stood in Jerusalem until 70 c.e.) would be paid out of communal funds. Maimonides comments that if the initial salary were not sufficient, the amount would be increased "according to the needs of the workers, their wives and their families."[17] On this statement, Rabbi Halevy notes that the workers must be paid sufficiently "in order that they will be able to focus on fulfilling their duties, without concerns about the needs of their families weighing on them."[18] As Halevy realizes, a person who is constantly anxious about the well-being of his or her family will not be a productive worker.

The Economic Effect of the Living Wage
Some opponents of the living wage have expressed concern that raising wages will result in a loss of jobs and will therefore hurt workers. Although this expectation seems to make sense in a basic supply-and-demand economic model, real-life studies have found that living wage laws do not lead to job loss.[19] In most cases, companies find other ways to make up for increased costs. These approaches might include reducing

---

15. Tosefta Bava Metzi'a 11:12.
16. See Rosh (Rabbenu Asher), comment to Babylonia Talmud, Bava Batra 9a; Rabbi Eliezer Waldenburg, She'elot u'Teshuvot of the Tzitz Eliezer 2:23; Rabbi Moshe Feinstein, Igg'rot Moshe, Hoshen Mishpat 58.
17. Mishneh Torah, Shekalim 4:7.
18. Halevy, Aseh L'cha Rav 5:23.
19. For example: Christopher Niedt, Greg Ruiters, Dana Wise, and Erica Schoenberger, *The Effects of the Living Wage in Baltimore* (Baltimore: Johns Hopkins University/the Economic Policy Institute, 1999); David Reynolds et al. *Impact of the Detroit Living Wage Ordinance* (Detroit, Mich.: Wayne State University, 1999); and Mark Brenner, *The Economic Impact of Living Wage Ordinances* (Amherst, Mass.: University of Massachusetts, Political Research Economy Institute, 2004). Also see Jeff

the salaries of high-level executives, reassigning money from elsewhere in the budget, or passing on small price increases to consumers. In many cases, businesses have found that higher wages result in a lower level of staff turnover and a higher rate of employee productivity. Paying more, then, can decrease costs in the long run.

In 2004, Santa Fe, New Mexico, raised its citywide minimum wage from \$5.15 to \$8.50/hour; and in 2006, the city raised the minimum wage again, to \$9.50/hour. A study of the potential effects of this increase found that businesses would experience a cost increase of 1.1 percent and restaurants would find their costs raised 3.3 percent. Even if businesses were to pass on the entire cost of the increase to customers, the burden on customers would be minimal: A \$10 purchase would now cost \$10.11, and a \$20 restaurant meal would now cost \$20.66. The relatively small increase in costs reflects the small percentage of workers at any given business who earn exactly the minimum wage. Furthermore, restaurants that began to pay a living wage before the ordinance went into effect and to advertise this policy found that many customers actively sought out restaurants that paid workers more.[20]

Conclusion

Jewish law establishes the guideline that employment conditions should follow "the custom of the land." At the same time, the Jewish legal tradition acknowledges that allowing the market to determine wages may sometimes lead to conditions that violate other concerns of Jewish law—namely, the obligation to ensure that one's workers can provide for the basic needs of their families. Thus the Rabbis permitted the community to interfere with wages and other working conditions.

Jewish laws about employer–employee relations are grounded in an assumption that full-time workers will be able to afford at least their most basic needs. In contemporary America, this assumption no longer holds true. The first step in restoring the intended work conditions, then, is to pay workers a living wage and to support local and national living wage campaigns.

Chapman, *Employment and the Minimum Wage: Evidence from Recent State Labor Market Trends* (The Economic Policy Institute, 2004).

20. Report of Robert Pollin to the State of New Mexico, County of Santa Fe First Judicial District Court, March 9, 2004.

Executive Compensation in Public Corporations
Michael B. Dorff

I N 2005, Occidental Petroleum paid its chief executive officer (CEO), Ray Irani, more than $63 million in salary, bonuses, stock options, and other forms of compensation. That means that Mr. Irani took in more than $170,000 per day that year. Therefore, he earned more on a Sunday spent playing golf than most families in the United States see in a year, whether he shot a good game or not.

Mr. Irani was not unique, though his pay was at the high end of the range. KB Home, Lehman Brothers, Lennar, Merrill Lynch, Morgan Stanley, Toll Brothers, and Valero Energy, among others, all paid their respective CEOs at least $30 million that year. And 2005 was hardly a banner year. In 2001, Oracle's founder and CEO Larry Ellison exercised stock options for a profit of over $700 million. That is nearly $2 million for Mr. Irani's hypothetical Sunday golf outing, making Mr. Irani look vastly underpaid by comparison. Of course, Mr. Ellison had earned those options over more than one year. Mr. Irani has managed to accumulate a fair amount of wealth himself, some $440 million in Occidental stock alone. Compensation packages like these led one commentator to describe excessive CEO pay as the "mad-cow disease of American boardrooms."[1]

What do public company CEOs do to deserve the kind of wealth that will make even their grandchildren rich? Mr. Irani may be very capable at his job; I certainly have no reason to suspect otherwise. But is he worth $170,000 a day? That represents over $7,000/hour, even if he never sleeps. Why do public corporations pay their chief executive officers so much? Scholars like me who study corporations have come up with three major explanations, if we exclude variations on a theme. These explanations all center on power: the power of self-interest, the power of group conformity, and the power of markets.

How CEO Compensation Is Determined
To understand these theories we first need to ask why executive compensation in public corporations is different from other high-paying jobs. After all, few people complain when a rock star, professional athlete,

---

1. John A. Byrne, et al., "How to Fix Corporate Governance," *Business Week*, May 6, 2002, p. 71.

or entrepreneur earns a fortune; why shouldn't the stewards of our largest corporations also be well rewarded?

Paying CEOs of public corporations is different because it is less clear that there is a true market in CEO compensation. Markets require self-interested buyers and sellers on both sides of the bargaining table. When a sports team hires an athlete, the team's owner wants to pay as little as possible, because every dollar the owner pays the athlete comes out of the owner's pocket. With public corporations, in contrast, the "owner" consists of hundreds of thousands of shareholders, most of whom own an insignificant percentage of the company. The power and authority to run the company, including the power to spend the shareholders' money in hiring a management team, vests in the board of directors. The directors usually own some stock in the company, but rarely enough to amount to more than a tiny fraction of a percent of the corporation. As a result, those who run the company do not own it, and the money the corporation pays to its officers does not come out of the directors' pockets.

Theoretically, the directors are chosen and elected by the shareholders, so they should represent the shareholders' concerns and try to minimize the amounts they pay to officers. The practical reality, though, is very different. Unlike most democratic political elections, corporate elections for board slots are seldom opposed. Instead, exactly as many candidates run as there are slots to fill. The scarcity of opponents has nothing to do with the desirability of being a director—to the contrary, directorships represent wonderful opportunities, as I will explain later—and everything to do with electoral mechanics.

Specifically, shareholders vote for directors at an annual shareholders' meeting. Because most shareholders own only a few thousand dollars worth of stock, they seldom see fit to attend in person, even if the meeting happens to take place near their home. Instead, shareholders vote by means of a proxy form. The proxy form authorizes someone else to vote the stockholder's shares at the meeting, in accordance with the stockholder's instructions.

The corporation creates the proxy form and mails it, along with some explanatory material and other information, to all of its shareholders. The corporation's proxy form provides shareholders the option to vote in favor of the corporation's slate of board candidates or to withhold their votes from any particular nominees they oppose. The form does not list opposing candidates or invite shareholders to write in their own favored choices. Withholding votes is rare, and has almost no chance of legal effect. Even well-financed and highly publicized "withhold" campaigns, such as Roy Disney's efforts to persuade Disney's shareholders to withhold their votes from then-CEO and chairman of the board of directors Michael Eisner, can at most embarrass their targets. The law of most states provides that the candidate with the most votes wins; there is no majority vote requirement. As a result, if there are, as is almost always the case, only as many candidates as there are positions, any candidate who receives at least one vote will be elected. Directors themselves inevitably own at least a little stock, so garnering one share's vote is not a difficult task.

The key to board election, then, is the corporation's nomination. Candidates the corporation nominates nearly always win the election. Nominees are selected not by ordinary shareholders but by the existing directors. Boards, then, are effectively self-perpetuating bodies, with little electoral responsibility to shareholders. They may, nevertheless, take their responsibilities to manage the shareholders' money very seriously. But the lack of a direct financial interest to do so—the kind of pocketbook interest every business owner has—raises a suspicion that when CEOs negotiate their salaries with boards, the discussion may not be quite as adversarial as it should be.

The Managerial Power Explanation

This suspicion is what motivates our first explanation of CEO compensation, a theory that has been dubbed "managerial power." This theory involves the power of self-interest. Managerial power scholars argue that the CEO exercises enormous influence over every board action, including the selection of nominees for the board. As a result, the directors, who want very much to remain directors, grant their CEOs almost anything they ask for in compensation. Instead of opposing each other across a bargaining table, directors and CEOs effectively sit side by side and conspire to give as much of the shareholders' money to the CEO as they can.

To understand why this may be true, we need to understand a little more about what it means to be the director of a large, publicly traded corporation. Directorships are not full-time jobs. To the contrary, public company directors typically devote around 150 hours per year to their corporations. Most directors have very demanding full-time jobs outside the corporation, often as CEOs of other public corporations. As a result, although boards of directors have the final legal say on corporate policy, they lack the time, attention, or incentive to take an active role in running the company. Instead, they typically follow the lead of the CEO and the senior management team who, in contrast to the directors, do work full-time for the corporation.

Despite requiring very little time or attention, public company directorships pay very nicely, generally in the six-figure range. They are also very prestigious. Further, they can often lead to other plum positions, such as directorships of other publicly traded corporations. In addition to the salary in cash and/or stock, directorships often come laden with benefits, such as health insurance, life insurance, disability insurance, and pensions. In short, this is the type of job most of us dream of: short hours, high pay, and serious cachet.

Once someone has landed a position like this one, it can be hard to give up. Although CEOs are unlikely to be pleased by challenges to any favored corporate policies, there seems no method more certain to antagonize them than to challenge their pay. As a result, managerial power scholars contend, while directors tend to support all the CEO's initiatives, they are particularly amenable to requests for more compensation. Opposing such requests risks CEOs using their power for retribution, including the ultimate penalty of exclusion from the corporation's next nominations list.

The Group Dynamics Theory

The second explanation hinges on the power of groups to induce conformity. I should disclose my bias at the outset; I was the first proponent of this group dynamics theory. Group dynamics does not take direct issue with the arguments of managerial power. Instead, it contends that managerial power tells only part of the story. Real-life directors are seldom amoral, rational calculating machines who act purely out of self-interest. Directors may be conscious of where their interests lie and yet still try in good faith to fulfill their duties to the corporation's shareholders. If we believe that directors are, if not angels, at least not thoroughly corrupt, how can we explain CEOs' enormous and rapidly increasing compensation?

The group dynamics answer comes from studies by social psychologists. Although there are several relevant phenomena, in this short space one—groupthink—should suffice to provide a sense of the argument. Groupthink occurs in groups that emphasize cohesion and consensus. Although these traits may be very useful in moderation, groups that take them too far may suffer from numerous decision-making flaws. Psychologists have shown that such groups consider only a limited range of options, tend to avoid considering seriously options initially opposed by the majority, ignore information that argues against the favored policy, and highlight information that supports that policy. Many boards of directors may well suffer from groupthink. Prestige and friendship both tend to promote the sort of in-group atmosphere that produces groupthink. Directorships are, as I mentioned earlier, highly prestigious, and boards tend to choose their new members from among the existing members' friends and colleagues. Partly as a result of that process, boards are very homogeneous, which also leads to groupthink by reducing intellectual diversity. Public company boards overwhelmingly consist of white, middle-aged men from privileged backgrounds who have spent their careers working for large corporations.

Groupthink may help account for excessive executive compensation by making boards more vulnerable to CEOs' arguments that they deserve higher pay. Groupthink boards may consider only a range from high pay to very high pay, if those are the possibilities presented by their leader, the CEO (who is usually also the chairman of the board). Such boards may also avoid considering the possibility that they are paying the CEO too much if that line of thought would bring them into conflict with the CEO and, therefore, with the majority of the directors. Finally, they may ignore any information that indicates that they have been overpaying their CEO, such as comparisons to similar foreign corporations or examinations of the growth of the CEO's pay as compared to workers' pay growth.

The Efficient Market Hypothesis

The final explanation contends that there is nothing wrong with executive compensation in the United States. This theory focuses on the power of the market, and it is sometimes referred to as the efficient market hypothesis. The argument states that running a major corporation is an incredibly complex, difficult job that requires a rare skill set. Few individuals combine the necessary education, intelligence, talent, and experience. Because these individuals are so scarce, they can command a premium price, much as a star athlete can.

Moreover, a CEO who performs well may add billions of dollars to the company's value, and therefore to shareholders' wealth. The typical CEO compensation of around $10 million/year—and even the pay of those CEOs at the upper end of the spectrum, like Mr. Irani—is well worth the resulting benefits.

Finally, efficient market theorists point to the incredible success of American corporations. If there were anything seriously wrong with U.S.

corporate governance, they argue, American corporations could not have achieved the global dominance that so many of them currently enjoy.

Moral Responsibilities of the CEO

Although corporate governance scholars tend to focus on how to put boards of directors more squarely on the opposite side of the bargaining table from CEOs, perhaps a more interesting question focuses on the CEO. Do CEOs owe some ethical duty to the shareholders to forego their own interests? Our culture seems to encourage us to pursue every advantage, valuing us largely by the money we earn and the power we wield. Should CEOs play by different rules? Or would asking them to go easy on the corporation undermine the competitive spirit that is vital to a free enterprise system?

The answer may well depend on which explanation for CEO pay we believe. If the managerial power theory is correct, CEOs may owe such a duty. Knowing that the corporate governance system is slanted in their favor and that the shareholders largely lack the means to assert their own interests, CEOs may owe a duty to refrain from taking advantage of shareholders' weakness. CEOs who ignore this duty might be seen as essentially stealing from helpless victims rather than simply demanding a fair price for valuable expertise. Similarly, if the group dynamics theory proves true, CEOs might owe an obligation to exercise restraint in using their power over the board of directors and, through them, the shareholders.

The issues are more muddy, however, if optimal contracting (efficient market) theorists turn out to be right. Then those who argue that CEOs should demand less pay run head-on into the core of the capitalist system, the notion that individuals' pursuit of self-interest produces optimal results for the system as a whole. In other words, reform advocates must overcome the idea that, as Gordon Gecko so famously stated in *Wall Street,* "Greed is good." This sort of argument is very difficult to make in a culture that measures success by wealth.

My own view, as I have already hinted, is that the compensation process is deeply flawed. Many public company CEOs have betrayed their shareholders by at least accepting—and perhaps demanding—dramatically excessive compensation. There may be no legal duty to exercise restraint. But CEOs are entrusted with shareholders' property, under circumstances in which the shareholders are vulnerable. As I discussed earlier, public company shareholders generally are not able to exercise effective supervision or control over corporate officers. CEOs are in this way very much like trustees and owe an analogous moral duty to pursue their shareholders' interests, even at the expense of their own.

A Jewish Perspective

If we were to look at this issue through a Jewish lens, we obviously could not simply look up "the Jewish view" in some classical Jewish source because the authors of the Bible and Talmud did not know about corporations, let alone those that are publicly traded. Still, the basic Jewish approach to economics articulated in those sources and later rabbinic rulings give us some guidance on this issue.

Specifically, although the Jewish tradition is greatly concerned with alleviating the plight of the poor, it does not insist that Jewish societies be socialist in order to achieve that end; quite to the contrary, from the Torah to our own times, Jewish sources assume that we are living in what we would now call a capitalist economy.

At the same time, as Rabbi Jill Jacobs demonstrates in her essay in this volume, the Rabbis were not at all reticent to interfere in the market to ensure that its practices were fair and did not have consequences detrimental to society. If those same classical Rabbis were living today, then, it seems to me that they would indeed recognize a moral duty for publicly traded corporations and their CEOs to limit the CEO's salary to a sum that is reasonable in relationship to the salaries of the corporation's other employees. Furthermore, the Rabbis would then likely take legal steps to make sure that both the corporation's board of directors and the CEO himself or herself fulfilled that moral duty. Exactly how they would do this would depend on which of the theories discussed here they believed.

Government Money

Michael Masch

G OVERNMENT PROVIDES for some needs of the members of society better than individuals could do on their own. This requires, among other things, taking money from people by law and force through taxation. Those who run government decide how much of the wealth and the income of various members of society government will take for shared public purposes and what those shared public purposes will be.

That is one of the reasons why we, in Western societies, generally believe that the best form of government is democracy, for we think that the people who are being taxed and thus being forced to contribute should have some say in how their money is used by choosing the people who make these decisions. This includes how much wealth and income is to be appropriated for public purposes. But what should those public purposes be? What should be the relative size of the shared, public government sector relative to the private market, individual sector? What should we do as individuals, and what should we do as a community through government action?

The Expanding Role of Government

Beyond police power, government manifests itself on many different levels. States focus primarily on educational and social services. We Americans have decided that it is the government's responsibility to provide people with the education that will enable them to be economically self-sufficient. This now includes college and even graduate education. We have also decided that for broad groups of people whose incomes are below a certain level or who are disabled we will provide services and supports that we expect other people to provide for themselves. This is especially true for those who have encountered some type of misfortune that is completely beyond their individual control. If someone has a child who is severely mentally retarded, for example, we have decided as a society that this is not just that family's problem. The state provides various types of support in the home and the school that otherwise would bankrupt most of us.

John Kenneth Galbraith, in the last century, pointed out that the 20th century was probably the first time in human history that we had societies, with the United States in the vanguard, wherein the poor were a minority. According to Galbraith, this meant that such a society could readily choose not to focus its social priorities exclusively on ameliorating and preventing poverty; it might rather choose to provide services to other segments of the population. Indeed, the sphere of government in our day is much larger relative to the private sphere than it was in times past. In part, this is because our communities are getting bigger and bigger. An ever increasing percentage of the world's population is living in highly urbanized areas with more than 1 million people. As a result, people increasingly expect that the federal government will provide public services that used to be delivered to residents by the province, state, county, or town. If only because it takes a structure of that size to deal with the scale of services that are needed—and when the federal government fails to fulfill such expectations, as in the case of rebuilding New Orleans after Hurricane Katrina, residents are outraged.

For the same reason, more things that were private are now public. For example, Pennsylvania provides 1 out of 7 people with medical care assistance, 1.9 million people. When such a large governmental agency makes decisions that affect such large numbers of citizens, individuals' preferences and values may be overlooked.

Evaluating Government's Effectiveness

Perhaps because governments nowadays are so big and bureaucratic, people feel alienated from governments and think that they accomplish much less than they actually do. *The Washington Post,* the Kaiser Family Foundation, and the Kennedy School at Harvard conducted a poll about government attitudes in 1996 on a variety of public policy issues. A statistically random sample of Americans was asked if poverty among senior citizens was lessened because of government programs. Of those polled, 39 percent thought that government had little effect on poverty among senior citizens. The fact, though, is that the creation of Social Security during the Depression and then the addition of Medicare, some 40 years ago, have clearly changed what it is like to live as an older person in American society. As recently as 1959, one out of every three senior citizens lived in poverty. During the Great Depression, it was the majority. By the year 2000, it was about 9 percent. I do not believe that this came about because of voluntary wealth transfer; it depended on organized social structure—that is, on Social Security and Medicare funded by money we are forced to pay in taxes. We take so many things for granted—among them, government-controlled and -maintained highway systems and air-traffic control—that could not be accomplished voluntarily and consensually. And yet about two thirds of Americans believe that the government is inefficient and wasteful.

Confidence in political leaders is even worse. About 80 percent of people believe that political leaders, once elected, are concerned about their own well-being and not about the people whom they represent. I call this the "quiet crisis" of confidence in government in America. We have a democratic society in which we choose people and give them power, and then we believe that most of them use that power in ways that are not in the broader public interest. Worse, even those in government who are well motivated and ethical may be ineffective, if a majority of people do not have a great deal of confidence in what they are doing. Schools should require a civics course to teach children what government actually accomplishes and how.

Repairing What Is Broken

Another complexity is that Americans do not have a broad consensus about how to repair what is broken. If one of our moral imperatives is "*tikkun olam*"—we should fix the world—the implicit presumption is that we know how to do it! If you lose the heel on your shoe, you go to a shoemaker; or if you tear your clothes, you go to a tailor—these people know how to make the *tikkun;* but if the issue is that some people are not economically self-sufficient, what should we do?

There are two broadly competing views: conservative and liberal. According to the former, poverty results from the failure of people to work hard and the expectation that others will support those who do not support themselves. There are some people who are basically willing to become wards of the rest of us in their indolence; they are willing to take from others rather than function as productive members of society. The best thing society can do is to refuse to help those in need to motivate them to change their circumstances, a goal that is within their power if they will only use it. Therefore, we should not give them welfare or income maintenance; they will not starve but will, with no alternatives, find work.

The liberal view is that people are poor through no fault of their own, and so we need to do something to help them. Then, however, that consensus breaks down. What is it exactly that we need to do? Is our job just to sustain them? Maimonides maintains in his Mishneh Torah that if people are going to starve, you first give them food. Almost everyone would agree to that. But then what do you do? Do you keep on feeding them, or do you do something else? I think that the presumption in the rabbinic sources is that people are in these circumstances through no fault of their own and they need help—self-evidently. In our society, we do not have a consensus about this. We certainly do not have a consensus about what to do. How should we enable people to become more self-sustaining? What is the appropriate role of the public sector?

One of the things that the Pennsylvania government developed recently is called "Cover All Kids," which we hope the legislature is going to enact. The argument from the conservatives against this program is that the more the government provides health care that is paid for through taxes, the less incentive there will be for employers to offer health care. When more people are covered by governmentally provided health care, more will lose their insurance. Thus it is a zero-sum game. In the meantime, Pennsylvania has 135,000 kids who have no health insurance.

My Role As a Government Official

There are two different levels in government: the people who are elected, and those who work for them. I work for the chief executive of Pennsylvania, and I am accountable to the legislature. I have to be willing to live under the rules and policies and the constraints established by elected officials to whom I am accountable. I can attempt to influence them by articulating my values, but my power is very circumscribed. Even they cannot do what they think is right if it is not popular.

It is not just a question of goals; it is also one of effectiveness and efficiency. To conduct yourself ethically as a public servant, you must not only want to do the right thing but you must have an effective strategy to do it and spend no more money than necessary to achieve the worthwhile goal. The goal has to be good, and there has to be a reasonable chance to achieve it, but you also must have a plan that uses no more resources than absolutely necessary.

Strategies for Allocating Money in the Budget

Beyond starving, there is a very strong tension among doing three things: investing for the future; meeting current needs; and not alienating the voters, who ultimately exercise the power to replace us with people who have a different agenda. The children of middle-class and affluent people are generally doing okay in school. A large minority of kids, however, one out of four, are not performing well enough to become self-sufficient and get a job when they grow up. But the majority elects governments in our society. If the way to gain adequate schooling for 80 percent of the youngsters instead of only 65 percent is to double people's school taxes, we will be voted out of office. We must instead try to strike a balance between the constraints of democracy and the clear moral imperative of those who take biblical and talmudic ethics seriously to ensure that children learn the skills necessary to be self-sufficient as adults. Short term, you give people food and clothing if they need that; but in the longer term, the goal is to provide people with an education and economic structure in which they can work productively, and, given that work, have a decent standard of living. It is both in the financial interest of government to ensure that that happens and its moral duty to do so. But it is not so easy to convince the public to allot the funds necessary to accomplish this. So you do what you can to balance current needs, investment for the future, and the willingness of the public to provide money.

My paradigm is not framed in terms of right and wrong, good, and bad; my paradigm is continuous improvement. The same questions about needs and allocations present themselves over and over again, but we keep working on them. I believe that this is a *tikkun* kind of mentality. Our job is not to will the world from its imperfect state to paradise overnight but to keep on fixing.

Intergenerational Justice

The government's power to take resources from people is actually an even greater power than most people realize. The government has the ability to borrow and obligate future citizens to repay the money borrowed. So we can require not only current citizens to make contributions to the public sphere that they may not want to make but also people in the future. This is a very awesome power.

The worst possible thing we could do is take money from future generations and squander it. Your job, if you are a responsible public financial manager, is to invest borrowed dollars in creating long-term assets. But not everybody does that. In New Jersey under Jim McGreevy, the tobacco settlement dictated that tobacco companies would pay the state every year a sum of money to make up for the fact that they sold a considerable amount of cigarettes that got many people sick, adding to the state's health-care costs. The state, though, borrowed a whole chunk of money against that future stream of payment to balance the budget in a single year.

That was an unethical thing to do. One should engage in deficit spending only for future needs. Paying for medications for the elderly today is a current expense that should not be funded by deficits. The war against Nazism, on the other hand, was a good investment for us to make for future generations because it was necessary to ensure the safety and security—indeed, the very lives—of free people everywhere.

Gambling

Gambling has become a government-sanctioned, government-regulated activity in the United States. Gambling is also going on in faith-based institutions as well. Judaism looks askance at gambling. Gambling makes one ineligible to be a witness in Jewish judicial proceedings (Mishnah Sanhedrin 3:3). The Talmud (Babylonian Talmud Sanhedrin 24b*ff*) has two objections to gambling: It may keep people from doing something productive for society, and it is akin to stealing, for nobody sits down to the gambling table with the intention of losing money. How, then, should I as a Jew approach what many states are now doing—namely, encouraging gambling as a way of raising money?

The reality is that people in society, without government intervention, will gamble. The question is how will gambling be structured? When gambling is made illegal, then criminals organize it. They do not worry about the gambling addictions of their clients. The only limits that criminals set on how much people will bet is how much they think they can get out of them. Government-regulated gambling monitors people's activity; and, if it is done right, those who lose too much money are escorted out of the facility. Moreover, we require that a portion of the money be spent on gambling-addiction programs. The Mafia surely does not do that!

If you assume that gambling is going to happen anyway, I think it is better for it to be managed and regulated by government. That way there can be some restraints on individual behavior, the odds are public, and there are some limits on how outrageous the odds can be so that there is some possibility to win.

There is another factor. Gambling is beginning to be offered in all the states surrounding Pennsylvania. The question then becomes whether we want our citizens to spend their money in other states or keep it here.

Even though I think that it is preferable for the state to regulate gambling rather than making it totally illegal, I do have a serious question about it. It is thought that lotteries prey on the poor who see this as their easy way out of poverty. Is gambling disproportionately practiced by poor people and thus just another form of oppressing them, or does it spread across all segments of society? That is clearly something that we must investigate.

Applying a Jewish Lens to Public Policy

Several problems arise in trying to apply traditional Jewish sources on ethics to our dilemmas in dealing with public policy in modern society.

The first is that we depend much more on government than did people in biblical and talmudic times. Many essential functions of daily living are now in the hands of complex governmental structures over which we have very limited direct control, and whatever control we do have is very broadly shared. That is, we get to vote, but our vote is one vote out of many.

Furthermore, the public structures that deliver services now tend to be operating on a much larger scale in geographic area and the numbers of people they serve than did governments in biblical and talmudic times. This means that each of our individual voices and preferences has a relatively smaller effect on how society functions.

Moreover, traditional Jewish sources do not assume a democratic structure for government. A monarch or a clan chieftain would have to wrestle with only his own individual conscience. In sharp contrast, the job of a public servant working in government in our democratic, capitalistic society in the early 21st century is, in very substantial measure, to implement the will of the people as it is grossly and imperfectly translated through the elected representatives who become the surrogates for everyone else.

All of this does not mean, however, that Jewish values are irrelevant to my functioning in government. The fundamental, underlying bedrock of Jewish ethics is that every human being is as important as the other, everyone is God's holy creation. As an ethical Jew, I am concerned about the fact that other people are living in squalor or misery. I cannot be unconcerned if I live in a society in which some people are enormously disadvantaged. It is clear that Jewish ethics does not require that everyone make the same income as long as everyone can afford to live. If some are wealthier than others, that is fine; but there is a necessary minimum, a level of dignity to which every human being is entitled.

That is my ultimate value, but as a government servant, I cannot exercise that value effectively in a democratic society if I alienate the political majority. After all, we Jews are a small minority in American society. So I can and should act out of the values and concepts of my Jewish heritage, but I must apply them to vastly different realities from the ones in which they were shaped, and I must do so in cooperation with people from other faiths and no faith. That is not easy; but it is not as hard as it sounds because the grounding Judaism gives me helps me choose my priorities and motivates me to attain them.

Money, Women, Children, and the Jewish Future

Fridelle Zaiman Spiegel

"MONEY MAKES the world go 'round," sings the star of the musical *Cabaret*. And, at the beginning of the 21st century in the United States, it seems as if he is correct. Money affects, and sometimes even controls, not only purchasing power but less concrete things as well: health, social status, and ability to run for political office. Although money cannot buy love, it can certainly buy many of the things that can help make one appear to be more loveable: good looks, a nice car, living in a good neighborhood. Money can certainly buy a private-school education as well as tuition at an upscale college or graduate school, assets that themselves command higher wages for those fortunate enough to acquire them.

Money as a Mark of Values
Although traditionally money is not viewed as a high Jewish value, it has certainly become very significant in the contemporary Jewish community. The often quoted aphorism from Ethics of the Fathers (Pirkei Avot) 4:1 is that the rich person is one who is happy with his or her portion. But it is expensive to lead a full Jewish life. Synagogue membership, contributions to Jewish causes, generally for the support of the State of Israel, are all required. And then there are the children. How can we give our children the best Jewish education if we do not have enough money? How can we pay for them to go to the colleges or universities that have significant numbers of Jewish students so that their chances of meeting a Jewish mate will be maximized?

It is even more complex that money not only offers people the chance to acquire many of life's tangible and intangible goodies but also tells us what our society values. Entertainers—sports, film, even newscasters—earn astronomical wages. People who make more money from money are rewarded. Physical strength is viewed as more valuable than nurturing qualities. Men are more valued than women. The bottom end of the wage scale is reserved for women who work with children—day-care workers and nursery school aides, with schoolteachers not far ahead.

And the Jewish community does not distinguish itself from the larger community in this regard. It takes a significant amount of money to become a *macher, a* respected layperson in the Jewish community. Even the old system of Jewish communal life, where United Jewish Appeal and Jewish Federations decided with their mostly wealthy board members how Jewish money was to be spent, is being quickly replaced by the decisions of Jewish billionaires who fund their favorite projects, whether or not they fill the most pressing needs of the Jewish community.

Nor does the allocation of Jewish monies give us any hint of traditional Jewish values. Trips to Israel are paid for, but only for those who come from weakly affiliated or unaffiliated homes. The experience of being in Israel is thought to be more significant than education—either education about Israel or about any other Jewish topic. Our teachers at any level of schooling do not get the respect that Jewish values would predict. Nor do they receive wages commensurate with their training. These teachers are usually paid even less than public-school teachers, and they are frequently offered no benefits—not even health insurance. Middle-class people are supposed to give *tzedakah* because it is a Jewish value, but the wealthy expect to get something in return for their contributions—a dinner, an honorary degree, their name on a building.

Speaking about money and values is quite a bit easier than actually putting our money where our mouths are. It is a lot easier to think about what our values should be than to actually live them, especially when it comes to money.

We often think of what we ourselves are ready to sacrifice in order to have more money. Is a position that offers more money but less free time for family more valuable than one that offers the reverse incentives? Is keeping Shabbat and holidays more meaningful than a higher paying job? Is doing work that you find socially valuable worth paying the price of a lower salary? Are you going to quit a job if your supervisor requires that you do something dishonest?

Comparable Worth

How often do we think about the larger implications of the variety of salaries and what they imply? Our society's salary scale not only decides what occupations should command more money but thereby decides who will have the status that money brings.

This is especially true in terms of the gender disparity in earning power. The issue of comparable worth falls within this category. Comparable worth, the notion that two people doing the same job should receive the same pay for it, regardless of their race or gender, became the law of the land in 1963. Yet women still do not earn the same money as men, even when doing the same job. And because women do not have the ability to earn as much as men, they also have fewer of the intangibles that money helps us acquire: power, prestige, *kavod* (honor).

There are many reasons for women's lower wages, some more value neutral than others. Even the more value-neutral explanations, however, show policies that favor men, especially white men. Jobs that require strength, for example, are more likely to be filled by men. These jobs tend to pay more than those that are associated with skills that women are thought to have. Any skills that seem to attach to mothering are little valued. Substitute mothers, such as domestic help and childcare workers, are the lowest on the wage totem pole. Teachers and secretaries are not well paid. And, in case you are thinking that these are value-neutral stances, irrelevant to gender, remember that in any wage category men earn more than women, even in those that are female dominated. Male nurses earn more than female nurses, waiters earn more than waitresses, and so on. Moreover, as job categories become more female dominated, they also command lower wages: think doctors.

Opponents of the comparable worth legislation argue that men earn more, even within female-dominated categories because they tend to work longer hours and have more consistent work experience. They generally do not take time off to bear or raise children. Nor are they usually the parent who is called to leave work to care for a sick child. Women who have the same work-related history as men earn wages that are a lot closer to men's. But not always. Women rabbis earn less than male rabbis. And, of course, as women rabbis increase in number, all rabbis may begin to earn lower salaries.

Men are also more rewarded for higher levels of education than women are. Women with postgraduate degrees earn little, if any more, than male high school graduates. In fact, in perhaps one of the greatest ironies of our wage system, in one study, women's greater educational accomplishments were shown to increase their husband's wages, but not their own!

The more that women act like standard men, the higher their wages. This means, of course, that women, or men, who take time off of work to bear or raise children are forever after penalized in their wage-earning capacity. If both parents work part-time, they are both earning lower wages, probably are both ineligible for benefits, and neither will be able to earn what a person who did not take time off of work is able to earn. And, as long as men earn more than women, they are unlikely to be the ones called for childcare duties and unlikely to be the parent who stays home as Mr. Mom. The system perpetuates itself without anyone seeming to notice.

Financial Implications of Having Children

Women are also far more frequently asked to make choices that rarely present themselves to men. To stay at home as wife and/or mother or to work; to work on a mommy track, being offered more time to achieve tenure, or to work fewer hours but without the perks of the fast track; to choose a career, such as teaching, that offers fewer hours of work and more time to be with children but less money and prestige. Of course, there are men, together with women, who make these same choices, but they are the minority.

Our wage system not only favors men over women but penalizes child care as well. Women who care for their own children are penalized by the wage system by not being able to present a consistent work history. Women who care for other people's children are penalized by their low wages.

Women who do not have children tend to earn more than women who do. There are very few women who are high-level managers and even fewer of these women with children.[1] There are fewer women than men in high political office; fewer women than men in high positions in the Jewish community. Men, on the other hand, are rewarded for having a wife and children. Married men earn more than single men. Married men are viewed as more stable; married women are viewed as less reliable. After all, they just might have children!

Households headed by women are far more likely to be living below the poverty line than those headed by men. Because women's wages are lower than men's, this statistic inevitably follows. And for divorced women the consequences can be even more bitter. A divorced woman's earning capacity is lower than her ex-mate's, especially if she had been a stay-at-home mom. And, very commonly, assets have been hidden in the ex-husband's name. A divorced woman ends up with less money, while her ex-spouse makes off like the proverbial bandit with more money.

Do we want to live in a society that favors not only men but the qualities that are more frequently attributed to men? Do we really think that raising children is not important, because that is what we tacitly assert when

---

1. See U.S. Equal Employment Opportunity Commission, *Glass Ceilings: The Status of Women as Officials and Managers in the Private Sector,* available at www.eeoc. gov/stats/reports/glassceiling/index.html#section5 (accessed Nov. 18, 2007).

we do nothing about changing the wage system? Do we really agree that those who educate our Jewish children should not merit health insurance, let alone a decent wage? And do we want to make it so difficult for working parents to send their children to Jewish schools because, even if they can afford the tuition, few Jewish schools provide childcare before and after school hours?

Valuing Jewish Women

Do we want decisions about the Jewish community to be made only by male billionaires or even only male millionaires? Is this the kind of community we want to live in? Do we want a community in which a contemporary Jewish think tank could find no women of enough merit to be invited with men to discuss the future of Jewish life? Our American Jewish community is changing because of money—both because of the high expense of leading a Jewish life and because Jews are ignoring traditional religious values in favor of American ones. Because money buys more than material goods, the potential results of just letting the wage system remain as it is, with its reflection of the limited value of women, has tremendous implications for daily Jewish life well beyond issues of respect, or power, or even childcare. For example, at the same time that there is an increased push for women to be more active in synagogues and, especially in the non-Orthodox community, to be able to participate more fully in synagogue rituals, we need to remember that women's participation, statistically speaking, lowers men's participation. Women, as women, are simply less valued than men, no matter what they do. Unless we change our thinking about the relative value of the genders, we may soon see not only a female dominated religion but one that is male depleted, one in which rabbinical authority is no longer respected because most rabbis are women. It happened in the Catholic Church already. The rules are all still made by male priests and their hierarchy, but the pews are filled with women.

Cynthia Ozick, in discussing women's participation in her Orthodox synagogue, noted that her synagogue was the only place where she was not called a Jew. There, she was relegated to the category of woman. As Ozick asked, can a community that so recently lost 6 million of its members really afford not to value half of its current population—namely, the women? I don't think so.

We already see the effect of the uneven value of women and men. If we do nothing about this, it will become even harder to lead a Jewish life in America. Yes, Jews need money to pay the costs of Jewish living, but

63

the nonmonetary costs we are paying are becoming too high. Can a community that says that it values children offer so little help to those who care for them and help to raise them? Can a community that supposedly values education offer so little scholarship money so that Jewish children can receive an extensive Jewish education? And can a community that prides itself on its Nobel Prize winners give so little thought to the future implications of its decisions about how their personal and communal money is spent?

Changes Necessary for the Jewish Future

To quote Ethics of the Fathers again: "We may not be responsible for finishing the task, but we are certainly not free from beginning it" (Avot 2:16). At the very least we need to pay more for Jewish education—in respect and in money. Teachers in Jewish schools should be appropriately remunerated and given benefits. More scholarship money should be made available for these schools. Our Jewish scholars should be given the *kavod* that they deserve. Just because they are not usually wealthy should not mean that their voices should be given less of a hearing than those on the *Fortune* 500 list. We need to raise the consciousness of the Jewish community to realize that the way women are treated within its walls has great implications for Jewish life outside its walls. And we need to train our children to respect women as well as men. We need to ensure that the synagogue and its leaders, both lay and professional, are given the respect they deserve, no matter their gender.

And, of course, each one of us—no matter how much money he or she has—has to weigh each decision carefully, with awareness that personal decisions have larger implications than for an individual life.

Money: Personal Issues

The Kotzker and the Nanny
Alana Suskin

R ABBI ISRAEL Salanter, the founder of the Mussar (morality) movement, was a *mashgiach*, a person who supervises kashrut (compli-
ance with Jewish dietary restrictions). His job was to watch the workers
preparing matzah. Once, when he was ill, his students asked what they
should look for while they were taking his place. He said "You know those
women who knead the dough?" "Yes," they replied. "You know that the
matzah may take no more than 18 minutes start to finish, and that this
is very meticulous timing?" "Yes." "The women work very hard for little money. They are poor. See to it that they are not underpaid. That is
essential for the making of kosher matzah."

This story reveals an essential truth of Judaism. The 13th-century commentator Ramban (Nachmanides) coined the phrase "*naval b'reshut
haTorah*"—a person may be a "scoundrel within the boundaries of the
Torah." Jewish law is clear that in every situation, God's directives require
justice, not simply individual details. Food is not kosher if the workers are
not paid, regardless of whether it was prepared correctly.

Yet, as Jackie and Ira in the third case study for this volume are aware,
this is not so easy. They already know that finding an ethical childcare
arrangement is full of potential pitfalls. Their options appear limited.
They want to try to find the most ethical alternative that will also meet
their needs. Jewishly, they are already doing well by struggling to find a
solution that protects the most vulnerable workers.

Anyone with children understands the desire to get the best possible
care for them. At the same time, the way that childcare is structured in
American society almost guarantees that we have to disregard someone's needs to get childcare at all, let alone quality childcare that meets
minimum ethical requirements for how to treat workers. In real life, how
do we untangle the difficulties?

Guidance from the Jewish Tradition
The process involves three steps. First, Ira and Jackie should recognize that
we can and should turn to our tradition to help us figure out which ethical
principles come into play. They already know in their gut that they need to do
more than the easiest thing. But how do they get past just using a gut feeling,

which is, after all, not very reliable as an ethical guide? The answer is that we must turn to Jewish texts. So what does our tradition teach us?

Judaism does not permit the underpaying or exploitation of workers. Jewish sources provide an extensive list of texts that underline how very basic the Jewish view of fairness to workers is. In the Torah, verses in Leviticus and Deuteronomy are the basis of Jewish labor law:

> You shall not defraud your fellow. You shall not commit robbery. The wages of a laborer shall not remain with you until morning.[1]

> You shall not abuse a needy and destitute laborer, whether a fellow countryman or a stranger in one of the communities of your land. You must pay him his wages on the same day, before the sun sets, for he is needy and urgently depends on it; else he will cry to the Lord against you and you will incur guilt.[2]

The Talmud, particularly tractate Bava Metzi'a, and later Jewish rabbinic rulings (responsa, *teshuvot*) and codes expand on the Torah's acknowledgment of the inherent imbalance of power between employer and employee and the attendant requirement to address this imbalance.

Still, one mishnah states:

> One who hires workers and told them to come early or stay late, in a place where the custom is not to come early or stay late, they may not be forced to do so. In a place where the custom is to feed [the workers], he must feed them. In a place where the custom is to give them sweets, he must give them. Everything is in accordance with local custom.[3]

This seems to imply that any community standards are acceptable. Does this mean that if people are using the large day-care facility or not paying the Social Security for their nanny Ira and Jackie may do likewise?

From the two Torah passages cited earlier, we already begin to see the underlying principles that must guide us. The Talmud states one must pay workers immediately. It elaborates on this as follows:

> It has been taught: "And his life depends upon it" (Deuteronomy 24:15). Why did this laborer ascend the ladder, suspend himself from the tree, and risk death itself? Was it not that you should pay him his wages? Another interpretation: "And his life depends upon

---

1. Leviticus 19:13.
2. Deuteronomy 24:14–15.
3. Bava Metzi'a 7:1.

it" teaches that he who withholds wages is as though he deprived him of his life.[4]

The Talmud (Kiddushin 17a) also implies that there is an obligation to provide sick and disability pay.

This begins to round out the picture. Although local custom is important, it clearly is not sufficient. It is also instructive to see how the Talmud (Bava Metzi'a 83a) elaborates on the Mishnah on local usage. It asks why it is necessary to mention that the hours of labor depend on local custom. It answers that it is to address the situation in which the employer pays them a higher wage than usual, because one might think that the employer can plead, "I pay you a higher wage so that you will start earlier and work later than usual." So we are taught that things go according to local custom so that the employee can reply, "The higher pay is for better quality work, not for longer hours." The implication is clear: Not only are workers able to command the minimum local standard in negotiating their pay but they are also able to state explicitly that if one pays the minimum wage, one gets the minimum effort. Clearly, although local custom might set a standard, it sets not a maximum but a minimum standard—to the benefit of the employee.

This in itself is an interesting point to juxtapose with an article in the notoriously conservative *Commentary* magazine,[5] which claimed that day-care workers simply "go through the motions" and that caring for children is not a source of pride or prestige for them.[6] Without addressing the nasty assumptions of this article, we can ask whether a well-paid childcare worker would be less likely to just go through the motions. Our own texts suggest that minimal salary will result in minimum effort for work and that that is not only acceptable but a reason for us to raise the standard.

Going beyond the Tradition's Demands

The second step is to understand that text is not enough. As Jews, we recognize that observing the letter of the law is merely a minimum standard. To do justly means to take that extra step.

---

4. Bava Metzi'a 112a.
5. Joseph Adelson, "What We Know About Day Care." Commentary 104, no. 5 (November 1997), p. 53
6. In fact, this turns out not to be true. People who work in childcare—as well as in other low-paying helping jobs—turn out to be quite dedicated to what they do, taking a great deal of pride in their work. It is thus a shame to denigrate those who do these essential jobs for us.

The famously cranky Kotsker rebbe commented on the tractate of Talmud Eruvin (21b):

> When Solomon ordained the laws of *'eruv* and the washing of the hands, a *bat kol* (heavenly voice) issued and proclaimed: "My son, if your mind gets wisdom, my mind, too, will be gladdened" (Proverbs 23:15); and, furthermore, Scripture says: "Get wisdom, my son, and gladden my heart, that I may have what to answer those who taunt me" (Proverbs 27:11)

He analyzed this passage by pointing out that King Solomon instituted many other practices as well. What makes these two special? The answer lies in their connection. The Hebrew *"eruv,"* is from the etymological root meaning "to include," "to be involved." Washing the hands indicates not only cleanliness but also holiness, separation from the mundane. This, then, is the great wisdom underlying this passage: to be involved and yet to maintain clean hands—that is indeed laudable.[7]

It seems fairly obvious that in the absence of their ability to commit to longer-term solutions for the day-care facility, such as organizing a union there or campaigning locally for a living wage ordinance, Jackie and Ira must take into account their children's needs first. This is supported by our tradition. Maimonides writes,

> A poor person who is your relative should receive your charity before all others; and [likewise] the poor of your own household have priority over the poor of your city; and the poor of your city have priority over the poor of another city, as it is stated [in Scripture], "To your poor and needy brother, in your land" (Deuteronomy 15:11). [Mishneh Torah, Laws of Gifts for the Poor 7:13]

Other texts also clearly state the obligation to care for one's family first. But in supporting ourselves first we need to figure out what qualifies as taking care of one's minimum needs versus giving ourselves extras at the expense of others.

Thus we begin by ruling out the large day-care facility. This facility both treats its workers inadequately and will not provide an acceptable level of care for the children. The other option presented by the question to this case is to take on a nanny but not pay her benefits or Social Security. But perhaps there is some way to work around the problem. Usually

---

7. Rabbi Ephraim Oratz, translator and compiler, *And Nothing but the Truth: According to the Rebbe of Kotzk.* (New York: The Judaica Press, 1990), 118.

what seems like a binary choice really means that one has not been creative enough to find another solution to the problem. For example, if two or three families were to hire the nanny together, it is possible that there would be enough money to pay for Social Security and benefits without actually overtaxing the nanny's ability to care for the children well. If this family were to ask my advice, I would suggest this and would brainstorm other possible solutions that might satisfy everyone's needs.

When I took my first full-time job as a pulpit rabbi, my family and I moved across the country, which meant that my partner had to leave his job. We decided that, for a couple of years, he would stay home with our son while I worked. We were able to make this work, and it was a great benefit for our son, who was able to have a parent at home all the time. Nevertheless, I do not think that I would suggest this as an ideal solution for Jackie and Ira. In Jackie and Ira's case, it is explicitly stated that they will not be able to put away money for their children's education if they spend much money on day care now. That does not even begin to address what could happen to the partner who stays home if the working partner is injured, loses his or her job, or dies. We know that a parent who goes on the mommy track continues to earn less than her colleagues—generally for the rest of her career.

Should one of them consider taking a position in another company that offers childcare to its employees but that pays less well and would offer much less professional satisfaction? That is certainly an option. It strikes a balance between the other possibilities and has the advantage that no one is out of work for good. In addition, by maintaining a work history, whichever parent takes the less satisfactory job always has the option of finding a job later, after the children no longer need childcare, that offers more fulfillment. If there were no other way to work out the kinks of the nanny options, I would advocate this last possibility.

Trusting That One Can Do the Right Thing

This brings us to our third, and last, step—namely, to have faith, not for others, but for ourselves. I do not mean this to imply that God will provide when it is applied to the workers but when we consider which step to take in a complex situation.

The tractate of Pesachim in the Talmud (118a) says, "[Providing] a person's sustenance is more difficult than the splitting of the Sea [leaving Egypt]." The Kotzker rebbe asked, "Why did the Talmud use the expression, 'the splitting of the sea?'" He answered his own question:

When the children of Israel went forth from Egypt, they saw the sea before them and the Egyptians pursuing them, and they did not know from where their redemption would come. One said, "Let us go this way," and another said, "Let us go that way." (*Shemot Rabbah,* Beshalach). No Israelite could imagine that the sea would split before them and they would thereby be saved. So, too, with regard to a person's sustenance: he thinks that his livelihood will come from this place or that place, while the Holy One, blessed be He, orders his livelihood from another source that he did not anticipate at all.[8]

To have faith means that when we do the thing that is righteous, God will help us to come up with the remaining provision for ourselves. It also means that we have to accept that we cannot know all the possible outcomes; at some point we have to make a decision and hope that it is the moral one. If we have consulted tradition, used its wisdom, and then gone as far beyond the minimum as we could manage, then we have done all that we could do, and the rest is up to God.

Modeling for Our Own Children

There is an additional factor that we ought to take into account as we decide between the various alternatives. A man once came to the Kotzker rebbe and asked for his blessing that the man's children would grow up to be faithful Jews.

The rabbi asked him, "Is this really what you want?"

"Yes," said the man.

"Then," said the Kotzker rebbe, "You, yourself, should be a faithful Jew. You should occupy yourself with Torah and take care to live as a Jew lives. If you do, your children will grow up to copy your ways. But if you do not, and you desire it only for your children, your children will copy your ways. They themselves will not be faithful Jews, but they will want their own children to be."

Then the Kotzker added:

This is mentioned explicitly in the Torah. Deuteronomy (4:9) says: "But take utmost care and watch yourselves scrupulously, so that you do not forget the things that you saw with your own eyes and so that they do not fade from your mind as long as you live. And

---

8. Simcha Raz, ed., *The Sayings of Menahem Mendel of Kotsk,* translated by Edward Levin (Northvale, New Jersey: Jason Aronson Press, 1995), 166–167.

make them known to your children and to your children's children." That is, if you forget the words of the Torah and do not watch yourself scrupulously, if you do not occupy yourself with Torah but only mention it in passing to your children, then they will do as you do, and only mention the Torah to their children.

Our ultimate measure is the fact that the way we act teaches our children. We should act beyond the minimum measure because we hope for our children to grow up to be decent human beings, and they will do what we model for them.

Strange Legacies
Sol J. Freedman

IN MY 55 years of legal practice, primarily in transactional work representing families, I have seen humankind at its best and worst. I am thankful that most of my clients have succeeded in transferring their businesses and their estates to their descendants with a minimum of acrimony. I have felt privileged to help convey a business from one generation to a second and sometimes to a third in an entirely harmonious manner. At times, I have seen incredible rancor and deep hatred within families—sometimes feelings that were latent all along, sometimes problems that emerged from the specific manner of the bequests—that I felt powerless to prevent. In such situations, in addition to being an objective counselor, I have found myself in the position of mediator, rabbi, and peacemaker. In some cases—particularly for widows with no family and few friends—I have even become the ad hoc personal guardian, taking responsibility for my clients' personal affairs. Along the way, I believe I have seen and applied ways in which Jewish values can ease the transfer of assets from one generation to the next.

There have been some occasions when I was confronted with clients' problems to which I could not find an adequate solution in the statutes, the case law, or my own personal experience. I would then consult with the late Rabbi Arnold Turetsky of White Plains, New York, who was knowledgeable in all the classical Jewish sources, had experience in life-cycle events and understood the dynamics of passing on property to the next generation. I learned a great deal from his keen intuition, his compassion, and his ability to bring harmony to the warring families.

Here are a few anecdotes that illustrate the very different ways in which people have handled the transfer of wealth within their families. Most of these stories, I think, speak for themselves.

1. In the mid-1960s, BH died, leaving his entire estate to his wife, DH. At the time, the estate consisted of AT&T stock, then worth $600,000, and a personal residence in a prestigious section of Queens, New York. The stock, alone, in today's equivalent value, would be $6 million (and the home probably $1.5 million). Five years later DH died, leaving two sons and a daughter. P, the older son, was then 28 years old. J, the younger son, was 26 years old. Their sister, S, was 22 years old. The will was probated within two weeks of BH's death. The following week, P called me and said, "Do what is best for my brother, J, and my sister, S. As you know, I was married several years ago and am working for my father-in-law. I have a super job using my talents, and I am being very well compensated. J is just getting out of medical school and will need help. S is expecting a child soon and her husband will be graduating from Harvard Law School in about 6 months. Do what's best for them." Two days later, J called and requested, in estate matters, that I do what is best for P and S. He said, "P pays income taxes up the wazoo and S's husband has no income and S expects to give birth soon. S needs the money more than me and my wife." Early the following week, S phoned and said, in my handling of the estate, I should do what is best for P and J. According to S, "P has extraordinary income taxes, and J needs the money more than she and her husband. S said that her husband just received two offers of employment upon graduation and has secured a one-year internship with a federal appeals court judge. After that, he would likely be offered a position as a lawyer in a prestigious firm at an unexpectedly high salary.

What to do? That very same day, I wrote a letter to the three children and advised them it was my honor to represent the family. I told them that, more than the tangible assets their parents left them, they had inherited a deep sense of love for one another that their parents had obviously instilled in them. In the graciousness and concern that they showed for one another, they had demonstrated what a rich legacy they were heir to.

2. NB, a client for many years, had an elderly mother who had been a widow for about 10 years. In her 70s she remarried a widower, who

at that time was in his 80s. Both his mother and her husband-to-be decided it would be best to sign prenuptial agreements to renounce any rights to the estate of the other. About two years into the marriage, the husband had a massive stroke and one side of his body became paralyzed. The wife tended to all of the husband's needs as a nurse, housekeeper, and companion for close to 10 years before the husband died. His two sons hardly ever visited their father and rarely spoke to his wife.

NB brought his mother to my office together with a will that had been prepared by another lawyer who had since died. In that latest will, the husband had written, "For the love and affection shown to me by my wife during my illness, I bequeath to my second wife, [the mother of my client] 25 percent of my estate [approximately $100,000]. The sons filed objections to the will based on the prenuptial agreement but were prepared to negotiate a settlement if the second wife would take less than what was bequeathed to her and if she renounced her right to become the executor. She was angered by the fact that the sons hardly ever visited their father and showed her no respect and also felt that the sons showed contempt for their father in not respecting his last testamentary wishes. She had worked as a slave to keep her husband comfortable with minimal outside assistance. In the end, the surrogate dismissed their objections and sustained her bequest. In addition, after hearing the testimony of the husband's physician describing the severity of the stroke and the loving care that the second wife gave their father, the surrogate had some unkind words for both sons.

Here we see a situation in which selfishness prevented the sons from doing what was just and reasonable. This tendency to act only on one's self-interest with little or no consideration for the needs or rights of others is a frequent source of animosity within families when they battle over an estate. Our courts frown on such expressions of greed and parental disrespect.

3. To present this fact pattern, we will use designations of "royalty." The husband and wife, whom we will call the king and queen, had two children. The daughter was the princess, and her younger brother was the prince. The husband of the daughter we will call the prince consort. The princess was the apple of the king's eye to the exclusion

of the prince and the queen. The queen was a passive, obedient, self-centered individual.

In college, the princess met a young man whom she wanted to marry. He was a poor boy from Newark, while she was a rich girl from the Five Towns in Long Island. He planned to go to law school, but she wanted to get married immediately and begged her father to give him a job in which he would make more money than he ever could being a lawyer. The king, who was a self-made man, had an extremely profitable business in which his son, the prince, was not active. At the cajoling of the princess, the king said that he would take the young man into his business but demanded that the prince consort work hard, for which he would be well compensated. He recognized the potential of the young man and made a further demand: that while the prince was not actively involved in the business yet, any deals that the prince consort would find for the business would be for the benefit for the prince consort and also the benefit of his son, the prince, on a 50/50 basis. The king advised the prince consort that he had given property to the princess and that that should remain hers. The prince consort would have to earn everything on his own and share it with his brother-in-law.

Agreeing to what the king wanted, the prince consort and the princess married. The prince consort came into the business and for many years was the active manager, while the prince, who loved skiing, scuba diving, tennis, and traveling, only occasionally appeared at the business. As the business grew, the prince consort, prince, and princess received interest in the business for which the prince consort worked very hard in comparison to the prince who was minimally involved in operations.

About 20 years after the princess married, the queen came down with cancer and the king began to pay attention to the queen, remorsefully realizing how he had treated her in the past. The princess never really got along with the queen or the prince. The princess was ejected from her royal throne and replaced by the queen. The queen loved her prince, who then was unmarried. There was little communication between the queen and the princess, prince consort, and their children. The king now started to bestow substantial amounts of money on the prince without providing equally for the princess, which made the princess furious. The princess told her husband that he was doing twice the work of the prince and that neither she nor her husband was being compensated proportionately. The king had more or less been in retirement for a number of years, allowing the boys to operate the business. With the hatred and jealousy the princess felt toward her brother, it became obvious that the prince consort and prince would not be able to work together; therefore, it was decided to split the business.

The prince consort asked me to represent him in the breakup. Their company attorney of long duration would represent the king and prince. At the end of the three initial meetings, I arranged a formula to split the business and divide the properties in an equitable fashion. The attorney for the king and prince and I had worked out what we thought was a fair settlement. The king approved it but wanted to think it over. The following morning, the attorney for the king and prince advised me that they changed their minds. What followed was seven years of bitter litigation. Into the fifth year, after the prince consort had left the premises of the business—taking part of the business with him as agreed by the parties—he died after suffering two years from an incurable, exceedingly painful cancer. It was said that on hearing of the cancer and death of his brother-in-law, the prince spoke words of delight.

And so, the widowed princess and the prince each continue to operate their own portions of the once-consolidated business. The three children of the princess were brought into the business. The eldest son did an admirable job. The younger son, who did less work, was thrown out of the business on several occasions. The grandchildren do not talk to the grandparents, and the grandparents do not talk to the children. In the end, this was the most dysfunctional family with whom I was ever involved. After seven years of litigation, the arrangements that had been worked out matched those of the initial three meetings.

In this case, we see what happens when parents do not treat their children (including children by marriage) equally, either in terms of what they give them or what they expect from them. When this is coupled with unequal levels of attention and affection, the result can be catastrophic. As I dealt with this case, I could not help but wonder how these conflicts might have been avoided and, once encountered, how much more easily they could have been resolved. In this case, too, the amount of money at stake was considerable. I learned from this that perhaps the greater the pot, the more venial the actions of the litigants. I saw that sometimes sibling hatred knows no bounds. Viciousness feeds on viciousness. Each sibling, in addition to trying to get a greater share of the estate, attempts to inflict more pain on the other. People are sometimes their own worst enemies. Most of all, favoritism fosters friction, which destroys families.

4. In the course of representing a new client in a real estate matter, I was asked if I could prepare a will for him and his wife. They had four children: two boys and two girls. The firstborn was an attorney working for a prestigious international law firm. The second child was a nurse. The third was a schoolteacher who, in her 20s, became emotionally disturbed and suicidal; on several occasions she was institutionalized as a great threat to herself. The youngest son was in his last term of law school. Their instructions were as follows: upon the death of the father, who had most of the assets, everything would go to the wife. Upon her death, everything would go to their children. Their dilemma was whether anything be left to the younger daughter who, in all probability, would be living with governmental support in an institutional setting or at least some protected halfway house?

The mother was adamant that the estate pass to the four children equally. The father wanted to exclude his younger daughter from receiving any assets because anything she would receive would go to the government. What to do? I explained that we could create a special needs trust with a minimum amount for the daughter to be held in trust for her special needs and that these assets could be sheltered from the government's reach. I then asked the parents whether the three healthy siblings would give part of their inheri-tance to their sister should the need arise? Both parents said loudly and in unison that their children would give their entire estate to have their sister healthy and normal again. I looked at the two of them. The mother started to cry—soul-wrenching sobs. Her husband held her. I remained silent. The husband then turned to me, then to his wife, and said, "I guess we will provide for the money to go to our three children. They will surely take care of their sister." The will was prepared and signed.

After the will was signed, I asked, "How is it that your sons are not preparing the will?" The parents answered that neither boy wanted their siblings or anyone else to feel that there was any undo influence by either of them in the preparation of the will. This was 10 years ago. I recently spoke to the father who said that the youngest son was now practicing law and the younger daughter was holding her own, living in a partially protected setting and gainfully employed.

When there is genuine love and caring within a family, even difficult issues can be resolved easily and without trusts or other complex legal instruments to provide for the unequal needs of the children. The law can provide tools for people who wish to transfer their assets in particular ways, but it cannot create compassion or generosity among siblings—only they themselves can do that.

I have learned many things from these clients, and others too numerous to recount here. And much of what I have learned comes down to certain basic values that I learned through my Jewish education—*rachmanut* (compassion), *tzedakkah* (generosity), and *sekhel* (common sense). These values are best inculcated by parents in their children when they are young. And modeling those values is the best way, perhaps the only really effective way, of transmitting them.

Most often, the estate attorney sees acts of kindness and love upon the death of loving parents passing their wealth to the children. This is so when the parents treated the children impartiality, taught them to depend on one another and to value integrity above all else. When children grow up feeling unique and valued for their unique gifts, they are secure and have no need to compete with one another or to take a larger piece of the estate to compensate for the affirmation they did not receive from their parents. In such families, children are taught the value of *sh'lom bayit* (domestic tranquility) and learn that they need to sacrifice sometimes for the welfare of the family as a whole. When children see their parents giving of themselves to the community, they grow up to become givers themselves; conversely, if they see their parents always looking out only for themselves, they grow up to be takers, thinking only of their own interests. It all starts with the upbringing.

Individuals are charitable when they see their parents being charitable. There is a truism regarding charitable bequests that we lawyers in the estate practice have: It is easier for a testator to think in terms of giving $1,000 if he has given $100 than to get someone who has never given

$1 to charity to give $100. On occasion, when clients have great wealth, I have assisted them in selecting charities by which their lives and good deeds will be memorialized. From my point of view and upbringing as a Jew, this is the ultimate kindness, a charitable act that is for the benefit of others as well as rewarding to the client and to the attorney himself or herself. Because I am in a unique position to know the extent of their means and to help them think about how to dispose of their assets, I believe it is my obligation in such cases to suggest to clients that they consider bequests to charity.

In my many years of practice, I have seen parents who have tried to rule from the grave concerning matters of religion, the professions their children will pursue, whom their children will marry, who will inherit, and who will be disinherited. Permutations of these defy the imagination. The wiser course is to let go, recognizing that once we have died those who follow us will have to live their own lives as they see fit. The time to influence our children and set them on the right course is while we are alive, not after we are gone.

In sum, those who succeed in transferring their assets to their descendants smoothly and harmoniously are those who see those assets as just part of a larger legacy, a legacy that should include a set of values by which to live. Absent those values, there is no end to the baseless hatred, irrational jealousies, narcissistic indifferences, sadism and masochism that people display toward one another as they vie for a piece of what they believe is owed to them. With the gift of those virtues—compassion, generosity, and common sense—children can accept what they get with gratitude, for they understand that they are the beneficiaries of a legacy that cannot be measured in dollars alone.

Philanthropy

From the Pragmatic to the Sublime—And Back Again: A Jew's Thoughts on Money

Jonathan Lopatin

T HE FUNNY thing about money is that it is a problem for those who have enough as well as for those who don't. It is a problem for those busy making it, for those who will never make it all, and for those who have finished with the give and take of the commercial jungle. The heart-wrenching challenges faced by those in need (and by any reasonable standard, this comprises most people alive in the world today) are abundantly clear to anyone with eyes to see the crushing effect of poverty all around us. But what about the issues raised for those of us who have more than we need to meet our own material needs and who feel obligated to share some of our wealth with others? In varying degrees, most American Jews today—from business people and professionals who lead lives of relative comfort to the mega-millionaires so visible in our philanthropic institutions—fall into this category.

Money is both a source of wealth and a medium of exchange. As such, where money comes from and how we choose to use it determines one person's good fortune and another's bad luck. Even if the fundamental problem of bad things happening to good people (in theological terms, the problem of *theodicy*) often presents itself as a question of physical health rather than of wealth or poverty, money makes a great difference even in matters of life and death—as Americans without adequate health insurance all too often bear witness. What more fertile ground, then, is there in which to consider the rightness of our conduct toward our neighbors than in the question of how to use money to help others? How much is too much? What special responsibilities does prosperity bring? Whom should we use our resources to help, and how should we help them? Can the Jewish tradition, formed over many thousands of years, teach me anything practical about this in today's circumstances, which differ vastly from the circumstances of the ancient world in which these values were originally formed?

Social Responsibility in Jewish Tradition

I recently heard Dr. Judith Hauptman, one of America's most prominent Talmud scholars, teach a group of rabbinical students that "Social justice is the driving force of *halakhah* (Jewish law)." This statement comes as a shock to liberal Jews who often think that the force of *halakhah* has more to do with *rite* than with *right.* But her claim that just conduct and the ties that bind members of a community to one another are as central to Judaism as theology and ritual should come as no surprise. Indeed, the complex interplay of our relations with our neighbors and of our duties to God is the subtext of many of even the most arcane questions of Jewish law. That is why practical people, who don't necessarily have a taste for the arcane, seek guidance in the traditional study of Jewish texts. If the prophet Micah (6:8) taught us to "do justice and to love goodness and to walk humbly with your God," the job of the Rabbis was to apply that dictum to the concrete circumstances of our lives; the Mishnah, the Talmud, and the rest of rabbinic literature are a record of their attempts to do so. I understand from this tradition that *tzedakah* is not voluntary but is a responsibility incumbent on each of us. Even those who themselves receive *tzedakah* remain responsible to give back to the community.

In this vein I find intensely practical guidance in Jewish tradition. Our tradition embraces the notion that people are obligated to use their resources to improve the lot of those who suffer misfortune, but it seems to accept the view that it is not our nature to be entirely selfless. True, other more radical practices were known in the ancient Jewish world. The Essenes and the Qumram community of the Second Temple period, for example, seem to have lived in primitive "socialist" communities, characterized by asceticism and the absence of private property. But these radical egalitarian social arrangements did not become the norm for Jews of later periods. Instead, although Jews have imagined an end of days in which society will function very differently from how it does now, we do not seem to be obligated to bring that utopia about *immediately* in our own lives. Instead, if there is anything at all that we can do to hasten that day, it is simply to behave well in the ordinary and concrete circumstances of our daily lives. Bill Clinton's promise as president to look after those who "work hard and play by the rules" resonates well with many of Judaism's values. How to do this, of course, is no simple matter and has always been the subject of intense discussion among Jews.

Instead of trying to erase disparities of wealth and income altogether, in the name of utopian perfection, my understanding of Judaism is that it expects us to seek to ameliorate the worst effects of the inequality that, in greatly varying degrees, is present in all human societies. When I pass a homeless man on the streets of New York City, I am encouraged to give him something—but I am not required to share my home with him.

In contrast to the modesty of this traditional approach, many Jews in the 19th and 20th centuries (including the forebears of many Jewish Americans) were drawn to the radical egalitarianism of various socialist, communist, and anarchist movements. Left-wing movements historically attracted disproportionate numbers of Jews—who often acted against their own personal and class interests. But Jewish socialists rebelled against traditional Jewish social values just as they rebelled against the prevailing capitalist order in the broader society. Even the kibbutz movement in Israel, while often strongly nationalistic, was a hotbed of rebellion against traditional Jewish mores, which were deemed to support an outmoded and oppressive status quo. The founders of socialist kibbutzim had nothing but contempt for substantial portions of the Jewish heritage that they inherited from their ancestors. And yet, one is tempted to find in the ideological debates of these revolutionaries and visionaries an echo of their ancestors' concern with the inherent unfairness of the world in which we live.

So each of us—even those of modest means—is clearly obligated to provide for the well-being of others *within* our community. But we are all members of many different communities. Are we responsible exclusively, or primarily, to other Jews, or are we equally responsible to the world at large? This is a fundamental—and personally harrowing—issue for many contemporary American Jews making philanthropic decisions. How much of one's resources, for example, should be directed to aiding needy people in Israel as opposed to providing relief to victims of genocide in Darfur who are clearly in more acute distress? How can we justify giving money to our local federation to support adult Jewish studies when the very same funds could be used to save the lives of AIDS patients in Africa by providing them with medications?

These practical questions, which determine how limited philanthropic dollars serve competing needs, are based on moral, philosophical, and spiritual dilemmas that go to the core of our conception of who we are— as individuals, as Jews, and as human beings. If we contribute disproportionately to Jewish causes, we follow a fundamental moral impulse that tells us that we have a distinct responsibility to other Jews that supersedes, to some extent, our obligations to the rest of humankind. Our tradition teaches "*Kol yisrael arevim zeh ba zeh.*" (All of Israel is responsible for one another; Babylonian Talmud Shevuot 39a), and Jewish fundraisers spend many thousands of dollars each year trying to persuade Jews to act in accordance with this dictum. They need to make this investment precisely because the validity of this proposition is no longer self-evident to many people in our community. Jews of this generation are much less likely than were their parents to support institutions dedicated exclusively to the well-being of other Jews. Many feel uncomfortable with making philanthropic decisions on the basis of what they see as archaic, narrow and parochial concerns.

Throughout much of history, Jews had little choice but to rely on one another for their physical needs. The reason that Jews bore a special responsibility to other Jews was, in part, that no one else took responsibility for them. In those days, looking after Jews in need was identical to promoting Jewish continuity. But this may simply no longer be the case—at least in the democratic Western world, where institutions of the state and of civil society care for most of those in need without reference to their ethnic identity. In the United States, therefore, Jewish philanthropy is increasingly devoted explicitly to programs promoting the continuity of the Jewish people *as a value unto itself*—to ensuring our *collective* survival when our *individual* well-being is not threatened. But should our sense of responsibility toward one another change if we know that Jews can endure as individuals, even though the Jewish people may whither away? Is dedicated Jewish philanthropy itself a mere vestige of an era when Jews needed special help to survive as individuals? If Jews now participate fully in the institutions of this society (in which other groups are far more marginalized than we), don't we therefore owe as much to our non-Jewish neighbors as we do to each other?

(Why) Does Jewish Continuity Count?

Jewish tradition abounds with sources that teach that the study of Torah engenders acts of kindness, so an investment in Jewish continuity is, in fact, an investment in our highest standards of conduct. But if our continuity is valuable insofar as we embody kindness, mercy, and justice, why not simply embody those values and let continuity to take care of itself?

It may seem strange to pose these fundamental existential questions in the context of an essay on money. But because economics is about scarcity, the issue of philanthropy and community responsibility inevitably raises these dilemmas, at least in the context of contemporary America. In fact, the "money question" inexorably leads us to pose, implicitly or explicitly, a very basic challenge to our communal norms: Why is the continuity of the Jewish people by itself a worthy goal? This question, which may itself seem heretical to some, is the elephant in the room of Jewish communal life in America today. We avoid it at our collective peril. Although we may not be able to formulate a single answer that would satisfy the entire community, each of us faces this question every day, especially when we follow our impulse to use our resources to make the world a better place. Perhaps it is time to make discussion of this question an explicit item on our communal agenda.

There are, of course, many reasons *not* to view Jewish communal responsibility as a mere vestige of a history of exclusion and oppression. For one thing, times change; our position as Jews may, God forbid, once again become as vulnerable as it was in the past. Perhaps we have a special responsibility to stay prepared for such a day. Even today, recent events in Israel and in Europe bring home the painful fact that the physical safety of the Jewish people cannot be taken for granted, despite the apparently exceptional circumstances of contemporary American Jewish life.

Moreover, our loyalty to each other as fellow members of a distinct community may not be entirely inconsistent with universal values. Even a dyed-in-the-wool universalist can understand that humanity itself has a stake in ethnic and cultural diversity. Perhaps it is simply human nature to create distinct cultures that bind us together in groups, which need not cause us to be hostile or indifferent to our neighbors. As an American I may feel an obligation to protect the culture of Native Americans—or of family farmers—even if these are not the cultures of my own community. Similarly, the United Nations invests in the preservation of aboriginal cultures around the world out of a commitment to human diversity as an end unto itself. Maybe the ideal of the "Family of Man" should be recrafted; perhaps the best metaphor for humanity is not a single family but an extended clan, composed of many families who can, under the right circumstances at least, live in peace and harmony. An investment in Jewish continuity, therefore, is also an investment in human diversity—something in which all of humanity has a stake.

But none of these justifications for investing in the continuity of the Jewish people entirely satisfies the needs of Jewish souls. To begin with, the argument that ensuring our physical survival is the *ultimate* justification for our continuity as a people implicitly denies any inherent, overriding value in our tradition itself. Without that sense of value, we are fighting a losing battle: Mere physical survival will ultimately prove to be a weak source of motivation. Approaching continuity as a means to save our collective necks may seem pragmatic because it appeals to our sense of the bottom line. But this approach not only negates the traditional religious understanding of the role assigned by God to the Jewish people; it also rejects *any* overriding imperative to keep Jewishness alive because we believe that our culture can contribute something to the world that nothing else can. After all, supporting Jewish continuity is not the same as supporting human diversity in general. Rather, it furthers our unique contribution to that diversity—and some manifestations of diversity must surely be more valuable than others. Supporting Jewish continuity ultimately makes sense only if we seek, find, and embody in our lives the compelling values at the core of our tradition. This may seem like a tall order, but it is in the deepest sense what our tradition demands of us. This, rather than mere survival, should be the bottom line of Jewish philanthropy in the service of Jewish continuity.

We are destined to live with the ambiguity of competing claims of many worthy causes. When F. Scott Fitzgerald remarked that the mark of an intelligent person is to be able to simultaneously hold two contradictory opinions, he described a type of intelligence that is highly valued in the Jewish tradition (as anyone who has ever looked at a page of Talmud can tell you). It would be too much to expect to find unambiguous answers to all the questions raised in thinking about our philanthropic obligations. The good news, though, is that Judaism thrives when we engage many unanswered questions around our communal table—not when we think we have all the answers figured out. We do know some things, though: We do not need to revolutionize human nature, but we must conduct ourselves justly and generously within the world. There is no magic formula to determine the best split between contributing to causes for the betterment of the world in general or for the Jewish people in particular—but we define ourselves by how we meet our obligations to both.

Jewish Youth Philanthropy: Learning to Give Jewishly

Susan Schwartzman

FORTY-FOUR San Francisco Bay Area teens sat gathered in the Jewish Federation conference room. They were awaiting a video conference hookup with six Israeli-Ethiopian teens who traveled to Jerusalem just to talk with the Jewish Community Teen Foundation board members. This was intended to be an informal dialogue, connecting Israeli and foundation teens. The question was asked, "What are you most concerned with?" The American teens answered, "Whether or not I will get into college." The Israeli teens answered, "Whether my friends and family will make it home safely today." There was total silence in the board room. This was an "aha" moment, challenging our teens to act in the world with greater purpose.

Hundreds of teens nationwide are finding such greater meaning through involvement in Jewish teen philanthropy programs. When they do that, getting into a good college seems a byproduct, not a driving force. What drives this new teen attraction to youth philanthropy programs? Like all people, teens today most want to feel that someone is listening and that they matter. Teens seek opportunities to exercise choice in the mechanized push-button society we live in. As our world becomes more automated and less personal, teens are seeking a way to connect around issues that matter. The technological developments of the last decade do not subvert a teen's need to feel wanted and needed and to have control and choice over important things in life. They do not want to live life tuned out, but rather turned on. Jewish youth philanthropy energizes our teens and allows the Jewish community to tell teens that their voices matter and are important to us.

For seven years I have forayed into the emerging field of Jewish youth philanthropy. In the past few years, due in part to the amazing success stories in youth philanthropy, there has been a wave of energy, including the recent launching of a movement. Hundreds of thousands of dollars are being raised and mobilized by teens for things that they care about.

The formula for success includes establishing coveted positions of teen power, offering teens incentive matching funds, giving teens training and access to community leaders and philanthropists, and guiding teens to make the final decisions that matter in the allocating of money to recipients. The Bay Area has been a mecca for Jewish youth philanthropy opportunities. Beginning in day schools, then in synagogues, and now in two new teen foundations, the Bay Area is working on developing comprehensive opportunities to interest teens in philanthropy during the Bar and Bat Mitzvah years and continue that interest through high school.

The Peninsula Jewish Community Teen Foundation (PJCTF), a 22-member teen board of grant makers, receives three times as many applicants as there are board spots available. As teens spread the word about their experiences, that number will double. We are drawing teenagers who are doing nothing else Jewish, Jewish-Russian émigrés, children of intermarried families, blended families, Israelis, Jewish students attending Catholic Schools, and Amer-Asian teens who have one Jewish parent. We also, of course, get those Jewishly committed teens who seek out opportunities to express their Jewish convictions by making a difference in society. We have unaffiliated, Reform, Conservative, and Modern Orthodox Jewish kids who are all working together and sharing ideas. Teen philanthropy attracts the in kids, sports kids, academic kids, techy kids, and the teens with no hobbies or affiliations. Each youngster learns that he or she has perspective and skills to offer to the group process.

We have teenagers who, amid their busy schedules, do not miss a single four-hour Sunday meeting. They seek Jewish information to learn about the community and the Jewish values that will guide their giving. What motivates their relentless attendance when they could be at myriad other places? It is the opportunity to be agents for change, to take matters into their own hands, and to realize that together they can make a real contribution toward repairing the world.

So what are the decisions being made by the teens, and what are the Jewish teachings that they are *using* to guide their decision making? The inaugural teen foundation chose to focus on hunger, the second-year group on health concerns, and this year's group on inequality and injustice worldwide. The board studied 26 grant proposals that arrived in response to the request for proposals that it sent out.

Board members dissect budgets, assess the resources and ability of agencies to complete projects, and determine whether a given proposal is a form of prescriptive or reactive philanthropy. They are learning about impact and reach as they increasingly become strategic grant makers.

They look at Jewish teachings, such as *kol yisrael arevim ze le ze* (All Jews are responsible for one another; Babylonian Talmud Shevuot 39a).

They study Rambam's ladder of *tzedakah*.[1] They find relevance in Hillel's famous quote, "If I am not for myself, who will be? If I am only for myself, what am I? And if not now, when?"[2] The text they struggle with most, though, is from Yoreh De' ah, where Joseph Caro suggests that teens take care of Jews and Israel before anyone else. "A person should give to his relatives before giving to anyone else. . . . [A]nd then to the poor in his own town. . . . [A]nd then to the poor in other towns. . . . [T]he poor in Israel should receive before the poor in other lands."[3] They look at historic systems of Jewish community allocations, but they think as universalists and see it as racist, selfish, or even elitist to help only or mostly Jews. This is how the majority think at the beginning of the foundation experience. By the end of the year, however, only two of the nine grants awarded by the PJCTF in 2006 went to secular agencies; 80 percent of the grant dollars went to Israel or Jewish organizations. This would not have been the philanthropic outcome at the beginning of the year. Rather, such an evaluation of preferring Jewish to non-Jewish causes comes only after months of learning, debating, researching, and—when possible—hearing the voices of the Israelis and seeing pictures of Jewish communities in need around the world. Support for Israel and Jewish causes is rare among the less Jewishly educated and the less serious Jews, especially at the beginning of the year. But the educated teens with stronger Jewish backgrounds paired with interactive programmatics led the group away from universalism and into the harsh reality that if we do not support the Jews in need around the world, there will not be anybody else who will be rushing to their aid. As one of my good friends put it, "If the Jews do not support the local synagogue, we cannot expect our Chinese and Indian neighbors to be paying dues."

There is quite a bit of learning that goes on in most Jewish youth philanthropy programs, but the most important thing they take away from their experience is that in this plugged-in and instant society, there are needs beyond their own. Moreover, they discover that they have the power and potential to identify and help fix the things that matter to them.

---

1. Maimonides, Mishneh Torah, Laws of Gifts to the Poor 10:7–14.
2. Ethics of the Fathers 1:14.
3. Shulchan Arukh, Yoreh De'ah 251:3. Caro bases this ruling on an early rabbinic source, Sifrei Devarim on Deuteronomy 15:7.

Can You Afford to Live in One House While Fixing Up Another?: Eighteen Thoughts about Money and *Tzedakah*

Sally Gottesman

1. My friend Fredda offered me the following definition of the word "wealthy": You have enough money to live in one house while fixing up another. If you are wealthy, this essay is meant for you. If you are not, that is all right, but you might want to start elsewhere in this book.

2. Healthy, wealthy, and wise. Are you all three?

3. I am a person with inherited wealth.
I am a person with inherited health.
I am a person with inherited wisdom.
I am very lucky.
I try not to abuse any of these three gifts I have received.

4. My father started a business, and it made him and me wealthy. There were many factors in his story—from individual drive to being white, from a great idea to long hours, from operating under a capitalist system to establishing himself within a reliable family system. In any event, he made more money than he could spend on himself, and instead of giving it all back to his employees, he chose to share some of it with not-for-profit organizations and some of it with his children and grandchildren.

5. If you can fix up one house while inhabiting another, you have more money and access to resources than 97 percent of the world's population. And, depending on how much money you have, you might be in the 99 percent category.

6. In theory, I believe that those who have money should share it with those who do not. But I do not share all of my money. Am I being responsible or irresponsible? Years ago, I read a story of a very wealthy woman who became a nun and gave all of her inheritance to the Catholic Church. I have wondered if her decision-making process was different from that of a poor woman who chooses to become a nun.

7. I try to challenge myself to give more money away each year. And so far, since the age of 25, I have succeeded. I am proud of this. I thank my

parents, my friends who talk honestly about money, and some Jewish teachings for this fact.

8. How should I decide how much money to give to *tzedakah*? How do you decide how much money to give to *tzedakah*? Many wealthy people have not thought about this question seriously. We may complain about being asked for money often, but are we budgeting for it?

9. Here is one way I think wealthy people should think about giving their money away. Figure out the total amount of your assets. Multiply this amount by some conservative to decent return. Take this number and multiply it by 10 percent to see how much you should give away if you were simply to tithe. Multiply by 20 percent to see how much you should give away if you were to follow the maximum that the Rabbis allow for most people—namely, a *chomesh* (giving away one fifth or 20 percent). For example, if you have $10,000,000 in assets, you would multiply this by 8 percent for $800,000. Then you multiply this number by 10% for a total of $80,000 and 20 percent for $160,000. These are guidelines for the amount of money you should (are there "shoulds" allowed in this realm?) be giving away from assets in any year. To this add a percentage of the income you earned in this particular year.

10. We ask people with fewer financial resources all the time to disclose the amount of money they have, including Jews (scholarships to day schools, synagogues, JCCs, etc.). We never ask wealthy people to share their financial situation so we can assess their *tzedakah* and/or spending.

Indeed, two things happen to many wealthy people when institutions try to move to a voluntary, sliding-scale system:

- They lie.
- They get insulted that someone is asking them how much money they have.

11. One method I use to give away money that I would like to share is the following: I have a nonwealthy friend in Israel, and I give her money each year to give away. No strings attached. She is on the ground in a place I dearly love, and she gets to choose to whom and how to give it away. (I recognize that I still get the choice/the power of choosing the person to whom to give this money, but there is something liberating about giving money to someone else to give away as he or she sees fit.)

12. Rarely at the Jewish Funders Network does the word "money" actually arise. Rarely is anyone challenged about how little—or how much—money they give away. Billionaires are lauded for their contributions of millions. And sometimes not even that many millions.

13. What is the smallest dollar amount you will write a check for? I am insulted when wealthy people send a check for $50 or $180. I do not even know how to thank them for their contribution. I am honored when a person who has less money contributes this amount.

14. I have friends who almost never stay in a hotel because it costs too much. When we talk about money, I learn a tremendous amount from them. They make choices I do not have to consider. I make choices they do not get to consider.

15. An acquaintance told me about a friend of his who had an elaborate, two-day 40th birthday party. It sounded like it was out of *The Great Gatsby*. He also told me his friend does not contribute any money to philanthropy. I wanted to know why they are friends. I wanted to know what his friend felt passionate about besides his birthday.

16. Over 75 percent of wealthy people in the United States say they will give more money to *tzedakah* when they have a cause they feel passionate about. Thus I think one of the most important ways to assist others with their *tzedakah* is to help them figure out what they feel passionate about.

    Here are some questions you can ask:

    - What articles do you read first when you read the newspaper?
    - What do you stay up late talking about with your friends?
    - If you could snap your fingers and solve a world or community problem, what would it be?

I am passionate about the health of the Jewish community, and I give nearly 82 percent of my philanthropy to Jewish organizations. However, my biggest dilemma is that a lot of this is transferring wealth from extremely wealthy people to well-off people. I know there are poor Jews, and some of my Jewish philanthropic money goes to help them. But a lot of it does not. Many of the organizations I support—including my synagogue and several of the organizations on whose boards I serve—are a form of wealth transference from those who have to those who have. I am at ease with this and not at ease with this, simultaneously.

17. Jews in America do fine, but not fabulously when it comes to giving *tzedakah*. I learned about tithing—for real—when *The New York Times* ran a series about families living on the median American income, which at that point was about $43,000 a year. I remember that in one interview a mother of three, who was the daughter of a preacher, spoke. She told how she tithed—and then figured out how to make ends meet . . . whether to buy new sneakers for her children or to save for their education. It was so very important to read this. Wealthy people have a lot more to learn from poor people about giving than from other wealthy people.

18. So where does this leave me in relationship to money? In the final analysis, I believe the way to use money for good—good for oneself, for one's friends, and for those one does not know—is to be passionate, modest, and generous in all areas. And those of us who can afford to live in one house while fixing up another—I think we have to recognize how tiny a minority we are and how financially lucky we are. And we have to act extra-humbly, extra-responsibly toward others. I am sure the Rabbis would agree.

Managing Money with Contentment

Sara Berman

L AST WEEK at my aunt's house, I noticed a weathered clipping that had been taped to the refrigerator. A woman had written an article in a New York–based magazine about her fear of aging, and on the refrigerator was yet another woman's published letter in response to this article. The woman in the letters column advised those who worried about the physical effects of aging to spend a day in a pediatric oncology ward.

"Aging," she wrote, "is a privilege."

For many days I thought about this letter. Yes, I was struck by the idea that aging is a privilege. But even more than that, I was struck by her advice. It certainly seemed true that the fastest way to wake up and appreciate the gift of growing old was to spend some time with children who are fighting to see their next birthdays.

This kind of response is embedded in the Jewish concept of *tikkun olam,* a Hebrew phrase that means to "repair the world." Through each good deed, the thinking goes, our world is brought closer to perfection.

There are many ways to view this central tenet of Judaism—this obligation to repair the world through social action. For some, *tikkun olam* is a way in which we try to model God's righteousness. Some Jews maintain that *tikkun olam* is a central way in which we have created our identity and sustained our communities throughout the centuries.

But that day, when I read the clipping on my aunt's refrigerator, what I realized was that *tikkun olam* is not just something as vague as repairing the world. At its heart, *tikkun olam* is about repairing one's self. Through social activism—volunteering at a pediatric oncology ward, working at a soup kitchen, tutoring an underprivileged child—we are not just improving the world; we are, first and foremost, improving ourselves. But what exactly does *tikkun olam* have to do with the subject at hand—money?

Whether it is Tevyah singing "If I Were a Rich Man" in *Fiddler on the Roof* (or Gwen Stefani's recent remake, "Rich Girl") or Cuba Gooding Jr. yelling "Show me the money" in the movie *Jerry Maguire,* it seems hard to miss the headline that having money makes a difference.

We have all heard it again and again—money does not buy happiness. And that is true—money does not buy happiness. But let's be real: I do not know anyone who would rather be poor than rich.

Money can buy freedom and time, which are perhaps two of the most meaningful assets. Having or not having money can sometimes mean the difference between receiving less than average or above average health care. Having money can mean the opportunity to travel to different parts of the world. Sometimes having money can allow you to spend more time with your family and close friends. Having money might even mean the luxury of not having to make your bed.

Those who say that money does not matter are naive. This is not to say that having money buys happiness, but having money can result in a broad range of opportunities, and nothing is wrong with pursuing those opportunities.

There is another practical reality to having money. It might not buy happiness, but it can sometimes—even fleetingly—help numb the pain of unhappiness. There is a certain coarseness to this reality, but nevertheless, a candid one, especially in this era of rampant materialism, where hundreds of millions of marketing dollars are being aimed by Nike, Apple, and Abercrombie & Fitch directly at young adults.

Few of us today are unaware of the ways in which these products momentarily entertain us and distract us from our genuine problems. A poll conducted in June of 2006 by CBSNews.com found that 45 percent of American teens have an iPod and that 67 percent have their own cell phones. Americans are learning about materialism at a younger and younger age.

In one of the most famous Jewish texts, Pirkei Avot, or the Ethics of the Fathers (4:1), the Sages ask, "Who is rich?"

Are all millionaires rich? Are all people earning minimum wage poor? Is an unhappy millionaire rich? Is a blessedly happy minimum-wage earner poor? If you have millions of dollars but cannot have a baby, are you rich? If you have millions and liver cancer, are you rich? Obviously wealth and richness are not the same.

The Sages answer that a rich person is someone who is content with his or her lot. This answer is as relevant today as it was when it was written nearly 2,000 years ago, *if not more so.* And I say "if not more so" because I think there are so many choices today—from the sublime to the ridiculous—that it is ever more difficult to be happy with one's lot.

At Starbucks, I order an iced skim latte with an extra shot of espresso. And even as I order, I wonder if I really should have ordered an iced mochaccino. Or just an iced coffee. Should I have sprung for the whipped cream? Or the chocolate syrup? Damn—I forgot to order the light version with fewer calories.

At Diesel, I try to find the one pair of jeans that I will live in. Will I be wearing flip-flops, low heels, or fabulous high-heeled sandals? The saleswoman wants to know this in order to determine if my jeans should be 30, 32, or 34 inches long. Do I want the summer weight? Or the darker, heavier year-round jeans? Do I like the distressed wash? Extra-low rise or just low rise? I finally decide on a pair, only to pass the window of Abercrombie & Fitch and wonder if I actually should have bought *their* jeans—or Sevens or Levis or Joes.

I turn on the television and have hundreds of channels from which to choose. Sometimes I flip and flip and flip, almost in a daze, eventually turning off the damn thing. Even if I find something I would like to watch, I cannot help but wonder what else is on another channel.

I want to get involved in a meaningful charity. I want to help children. I begin my search on the Internet. I see there are thousands of charities dedicated to improving the lives of children. Should I work locally in my city? Should I join a campaign to raise the awareness level of the millions of child refugees in Africa? How do I choose the right organization?

No matter what choice I make in any of these decisions, I am always plagued by this gnawing sense of not having explored a full range of choices. What did I miss? Did I make the right decision?

And sometimes it is hard for us to make choices at all. Overwhelmed by the range of desirable products and the ever-present game of keeping up with the Joneses, many of us overextend ourselves financially. Almost 10 percent of American teenagers have credit cards, and at 18 or 19 years old that percentage doubles, according to a poll conducted in 2006 by Junior Achievement. Alarmingly, only 15.7 percent of teens who own credit cards make the minimum payment. And so it is no surprise that a 2006 Senate report revealed that the largest group of bankruptcy filers in this country are 25 years old and younger.

It is scary, but it is important to remember that it takes more than nine years of making minimum payments and almost $2,000 in interest fees to pay off a $1,000 balance on a credit card with an 18 percent annual interest rate. The appeal of materialism, and the pressure exerted by credit card companies to capitalize on this materialist instinct have serious consequences.

Believe it or not, *tikkun olam* is a practical way in which we can respond to something as contemporary as this raging materialism and an overabundance of choice. Being determined to actively improve yourself and the world around you will give you the perspective you need as a constant reminder that wealth and materialism are not the same thing as riches.

My friend calls her weekly, two-hour visit to a hospital to visit sick patients her reality check. "It is so easy to forget the important things in our lives. I get annoyed when I have to wait an extra 20 minutes for something that I thought would take 5. I am vaguely aware of feeling jealous of my friend's new apartment. I flip through a magazine and want a new bag and a pair of jeans. The models are so thin. I think I need to lose weight. For the day or two after my hospital visit I know—and I mean *know*—that none of that stuff matters. And then for the next day or two after that I am still pretty sure that clothes and the latest accessories do not matter. By day five or six, though, I begin to think about that stuff again. Thank God for the visits."

She is not alone in her experience. "Once a month a friend and I volunteer in a homeless shelter," another friend told me. "Sure, the people who run the shelter need the volunteers; but even more, I am convinced that we need this weekly reminder of what matters and what does not. I work in the financial industry where money is the only bottom line. And I am fine with that. I am as competitive as the next person. But sometimes I lose perspective and forget that while at my job money might be the bottom line, in my broader life, money is just one of *many* bottom lines."

It is so difficult to strike a balance when it comes to money. It is easy to feel as if you are selling your soul by making wealth a priority: "I came out of college and busted my ass for five years," a friend now in her 30s recalls. "I was ambitious and hungry and a perfectionist. My friends from college acted as if I had become some sneaky, underhanded criminal. They were doing work that I viewed as equally important to my interest in companies—they were teachers and working in nonprofits and earning much, much less than I did. They struggled to make ends meet. But sometimes I wanted to tell them their work was no more noble than mine, just because they were paid less."

And on the flip side, another friend, now in her 40s, who had worked for a number of charitable organizations recalls with frustration how hard she worked for many years and received what she felt was inequitable payment. "I always knew my work was important, and I loved what I did, but sometimes I could not help but get frustrated when I saw how much some of my friends were paid. Even when you are passionate about your work, money has a way of defining you—unless you actively work to fight that from happening. And you must work to stop it. Because money matters, just not as much as other things."

By insisting that your life is varied and multifaceted—and by always making the time for some form of social activism—for *tikkun olam*—you will increase your odds of having a more comfortable relationship with your job, your friends, your family, and of course, your money.

Just like materialism, this kind of inner calm is also contagious. When you engage in *tikkun olam,* you will not only be repairing yourself and the world, but the chances are that you will also be serving as a beacon to those around you who are also searching for a similar kind of ease with themselves.

Examining a question posed in Pirkei Avot thousands of years ago, and recognizing its relevance today, explains, in part, the success of Judaism itself. Today—just like so many centuries ago—we want to know the secrets to being content. And engaging in *tikkun olam* is one of them.

Reflections on the Case Studies
The Price of Menschlichkeit: A Meditation on Money and Morality
David A. Teutsch

The First Case Study

JEWISH TRADITION teaches that a good name is a possession to be valued very highly. Once one sullies one's name, it is extraordinarily difficult to get it clean—it takes years of morally exemplary living to accomplish that task. Integrity—and being honest with oneself (*dover emet bilvavo*)—are central parts of maintaining a good name, as is living by the values to which one is committed. Our relationships and organizational associations are also important. As Pirkei Avot (2:9)—a part of the Mishnah that dispenses moral advice puts it—we should keep ourselves far from bad companions.

When selecting a place to work, the issue raised in the first case study in this volume, key considerations include the tasks that would be assigned, the people who would be co-workers; the possibilities of advancement, and, of course, the compensation. One of the problems with working in a place that has an immoral purpose, such as marketing cigarettes, is that the people who do it must either be morally misguided or self-deceived or both. That certainly raises the problem of bad companions. Studies show that most people conform to the morality of the culture in which they find themselves. You may have doubts before you decide to go to work for a tobacco company, but it is human nature to gradually accept the values and practices of the organizational culture in which you find yourself. One reason to avoid bad companions is that each day with them you lose track of your higher self a little more. From my perspective that is too high a price to pay for a job, unless the alternative is to be unable to provide food and clothing for myself and those dependent on me.

One way I think about this is by realizing that I have an obligation to reprove (*tokhehah*—see Leviticus 19:17) others when I see them doing something wrong. Most people understand silence to be consent, so if I do not offer criticism in the face of wrongdoing, my silence makes me complicit. To make that criticism effective, I should offer it in a gentle, thoughtful, and caring way. Some companies mistreat employees or produce shoddy goods as part of their basic way of doing things. If I go to work for such a firm and I protest the way they do business, I will be fired. If I do not protest, I will be complicit in that wrongdoing. If I stay long enough, being complicit will corrupt part of my morals—again, too high a price to pay for a job. One test of a good work environment is whether I can offer *tokhehah* there safely. If not, I should consider leaving while I still recognize that *tokhehah* is needed!

Ellen and Frank may not be able to earn money and advance professionally at the same rate if they do not take jobs with the tobacco company or sweatshop garment manufacturer. But living a life of integrity has its own rewards. Such able people will figure out a way to meet their familial obligations and give *tzedakah,* while hanging on to their good names. Jewish tradition teaches that even people so poor that they are themselves recipients of *tzedakah* have an obligation to give *tzedakah.*[1] Everyone can give something. Committing immoral acts so that one can live better and give more to charity cannot be justified Jewishly.

Central to the idea of work is *kavod,* "dignity or honor." We work not just to put food on the table but also to make our lives productive and meaningful. We produce value in the world through manufacturing, direct service, helping to make goods available to those who need them or sustaining the financial mechanisms on which our society depends. Producing value brings a sense of accomplishment and self-esteem, a sense of *kavod.* Employers have an obligation to treat employees with dignity; and just as important, employees have an obligation to do an honest day's work for their employer. Even when employer and employee act with *kavod* in this way, little *kavod* results if the work is not fully moral. One test of the morality of the work is whether it provides added value for all the stakeholders involved—employer, employees, customers, and venders as well as those indirectly affected.

Jewish teaching about work and about commercial transactions is concerned not only with *kavod* but also with building and preserving relationships. Jewish sources place considerable stress on using honest weights and measures, on not charging more than fair market price, and on honoring contracts. Taking such measures builds trust and creates an environment in which business is done cooperatively. If I want to enter into a contract, I should look to ensure that it benefits both sides. Recently I talked to the CEO of a large corporation who had just released

---

1. Babylonian Talmud Bava Kamma 91a; Babylonian Talmud Gittin 7b; Mishneh Torah, Laws of Gifts to the Poor 7:5; Shulchan Arukh, Yoreh De'ah 248:1, 251:12.

a vendor from a contract that was extremely beneficial to the corporation. When I asked why, the CEO explained that both sides had entered into the long-term agreement willingly because it appeared to be mutually beneficial, but that market conditions had changed so much that honoring the contract would have driven the vender into bankruptcy. The CEO said that it would have therefore been legal but dishonorable to hold the vender to the contract, which they replaced with one that had fairer terms. Jewish tradition refers to "going beyond the law in order to do what is right" as *lifnim meshurat hadin*.[2] The CEO and vender can anticipate working together in trust and harmony for many more years. This business leader profoundly understands the cooperative nature of the business enterprise and the satisfactions that come from exemplary behavior.

The Second Case Study

In the second case study, Jennifer entered into a contract when she borrowed money on her credit cards. She either understood the terms of those contracts, or she should have investigated and reached an understanding before she used them. She should have been able to look ahead and see the size of monthly payments she would be incurring and the amount she would have to earn to afford them. Jennifer could have left school and gone to work. She could have reduced her course load and worked more hours. She perhaps could have lived more frugally. Instead, she willingly borrowed the money with the implications clearly known, so she has only herself to blame. If she does not do her utmost to repay the debt, she is guilty not just of violating a contract but of a form of theft. That is the case from a moral perspective even if there are not convenient legal means to collect Jennifer's debt because of the expense of chasing her as she moves from place to place. Shirking an obligation does not make that obligation go away.

What are Jennifer's choices? She can negotiate better terms with her creditors. Most creditors are willing to do this because slow repayment is better for them than bad debts, and certainly better than forcing Jennifer into bankruptcy. Jennifer could also consolidate her loans at a reduced rate of interest so that she has a single, lower payment to make each month. If Jennifer cannot do this by herself, there are many organizations that are set up to help people like her. If the debt then stretches

---

2. For example, Babylonian Talmud Bava Kamma 99b, 100a; Babylonian Talmud Bava Metzi'a 24b, 30b.

out too far into the future, Jennifer can decide to work overtime or find a part-time job to supplement her income so that she can pay down the debt more quickly. Meantime, she should think seriously about canceling her current credit cards until she has repaid her debt.

What of the credit card companies? Is their conduct predatory? In Jewish terms, does it constitute *ona'ah,* unfair exploitation through overcharging? Generally, lenders legitimately charge higher interest when their loans are more at risk. Lending to young people with little in the way of collateral and short credit histories is a risky business, so to some extent, higher interest rates are justified. But there are certainly limits to this. One reason why government-guaranteed student loans exist is to provide low-interest borrowing. If the terms of borrowing were legally predatory, Jennifer would have recourse through government regulators and the courts. But if the loan rates were simply high because of the cost of marketing and the likelihood of loss, and if Jennifer was not coerced into borrowing, these lenders were within their rights, though I would not want to be their employee. In any case, the time for Jennifer to have protested was years earlier when she first started to borrow. Now it is up to Jennifer to do the right thing, and up to her friends to do *tokhehah* by telling her so.

Part of what this case illustrates is the complex interaction among facts, alternative actions, potential outcomes, and moral judgments. While some things are always wrong—it is never acceptable to commit unprovoked murder—many potential actions require careful analysis to determine their morality. Questions about money and business are usually of this type. Determining the facts of the situation along with potential alternative courses of action and their effects generally should precede moral consideration. The moral situation is different if the facts are different, and it is also different if the alternative courses of action are different. Sometimes a third party can suggest a course of action that eliminates the moral dilemma or simplifies it enough so that the answer is obvious. As I suggested, Jennifer's choices are not limited to ruining her life or refusing to pay. Moral analysis only works when it can utilize an accurate description of the available choices. Jennifer should be able to hold on to her integrity and her good name while gradually working her way out of debt.

The Third Case Study

The third case, involving the need for childcare for the children of Ira and Jackie, demonstrates complex interactions among elements and the need to step back and think about other alternatives. Breaking the law involves the violation of a fundamental Jewish precept of *dina d'malkhuta dina*, "the law of the country we are in is binding on us as law." Raising children is a sacred responsibility, and we are obliged to ensure their safety and wellbeing, so putting them in a situation where their caregivers are unreliable is clearly not acceptable if there are better alternatives available. What are the other choices here? Is there a Jewish nursery school in the neighborhood that can provide part of the solution? Can Ira and Jackie open their home to a college student who would trade baby-sitting for room and board? Can they arrange to bring in an au pair for a year from another country, an arrangement far less expensive than a nanny? Is there a co-op option available if one of them works somewhat less or they rotate work hours? Are their parents or other relatives available to help?

Americans think of the individual as the sovereign social unit and the nuclear family as needing to fend for itself. The Jewish approach is to think more in terms of an interdependent community and, where possible, extended family. The dilemma that Ira and Jackie are facing grows out of very high expectations regarding income, lifestyle, and job satisfaction, and low expectations about how a network of relationships could ease their dilemma. What matters most to Ira and Jackie? What are they willing to give up? To what agencies can they turn for advice and help? Their situation is not primarily a question of money. It is one of balancing complex moral goods and costs, and their best solution may well require them to rethink their priorities. Living simpler and spending more time with their children may turn out to be more valuable than saving for their children's future educations. Well-nurtured children will usually manage to make their way through the world.

Money is often a stand-in for other things of value. If I do not have time to mow the lawn, I can use money to hire someone. If I want to work less hard, I can sell my large house, move into a small one that costs far less to maintain, and take a cut in salary. In thinking about the moral aspect of financial issues, it is critically important that we not lose track of the nonfinancial ones. Cutting the lawn, living in a smaller house, and working fewer hours are extrinsic—they are outside of me and subject to measure and comparison. What is intrinsic, solely inside of me, is not so easily subject to measure. Integrity, *kavod*, a good name, the satisfaction of having a good relationship with my children and the warm feelings that come from good relationships with colleagues, neighbors and friends are all intrinsic.

We live in a market-driven society that at every turn urges us to value the extrinsic over the intrinsic. The resulting tragedy is that many people focus on owning and consuming as the main road to a good life. While it is certainly true that real privation can prevent people from leading good lives, once our basic needs are met, the primary sources of meaning in our lives are intrinsic rather that extrinsic. If achieving a career or financial goal comes at a high price in terms of intrinsic goods, in general our culture would say it is worth it. Jewish tradition would not. The things of highest value cannot be bought. When we trade them for money, we have sold out.

In my opinion, the ultimate Jewish compliment is to call someone a *mensch*. For a *mensch,* a promise is a sacred trust. Having the courage to stand up for what is right and the gentleness to look out for the feelings of others are all part of *menschlichkeit.* One of the signs of a *mensch* is that he or she understands that money is not an end or a method of keeping score. It is a tool for doing good and doing right in the world. Aspiring to *menschlichkeit* is a wonderful step toward creating a good name.

Money, Meaning, and Happiness
Zachary Teutsch

MORAL QUESTIONS cannot be easily decontextualized, so I will start with some of my story to show you where I am coming from.

My Own Approach to Money: Practical and Jewish Concerns

My senior year of college, like most, involved beginning to consider more seriously what I would do after graduation. I believed deeply that I had an obligation to change the world for the better, but unfortunately there were several companies in that business. Some business people told me that I could change the world more in a day as a successful business person than I could in a year as a nonprofit worker. Some friends in the nongovernmental organization (NGO) world warned me of the moral implications of going that route and all the wrong I would have to do for a chance to do some good. These many voices echoed in my head. After much thought I donned a suit, cut my hair, and began interviewing with investment banks, hedge funds, and strategic consulting firms. I hoped I would learn some valuable skills in the few years I would work in that world and then apply them to social and economic justice problems. I got several offers, but in the end I could not imagine going to work everyday for a firm whose mission I did not believe in. I had received a very good education, was relatively debt free, and was in a lucky position to allow that voice of conscience to win out. I ended up joining the labor movement as an analyst and am tremendously glad I made that decision. I think there are many other decisions that are moral, perhaps more moral than the one I made. I admire people who can toil in the business world and constantly keep their eyes toward the good of people in need. One of my favorite passages in the Bible says that the righteous walk in God's paths.[1] I like the passage so much because it talks about paths rather than a path. It is the same with choosing work, choosing how to spend money, and how to make the world a more just, holier place. There are many paths.

There are two major approaches I use in thinking about money, income, choosing work, and making financial decisions. One is a practical approach that comes from my time spent studying social science, and the other is a Jewish moral approach. Luckily, the two inform each other quite nicely. Practically speaking, it is important to consider how money

---

1. Hosea 14:10.

functions and the conditions under which it makes us happier or less happy. Jewishly, we must also consider the well-being of others and the moral implications of the way we use money.

A business executive, wanting a different sort of vacation, hired a fishing boat to take him out on the sea. They sailed, they fished, and the executive was more relaxed than he had been in years. One evening the business person said to the fisherman, "Why don't you franchise?"

"Why would I want to do that?" replied the fisherman.

"You could have dozens of boats giving fantastic fishing tours in many cities," answered the executive.

"So what?" responded the fisherman.

"You could make millions of dollars! Think of what you could do with all that money!" exclaimed the executive.

"I would sail out on the sea, put my feet up, open a bottle of wine, and watch the sunset," said the fisherman. With that, the fisherman put up his feet, poured a glass of wine, and watched the sun set.

The executive understood.

This story helped crystallize my thinking about ambition and wealth. We so often have the impulse to make things bigger and better so that we can be wealthier and more powerful. We rarely ask ourselves, *for what?* Wealth and power are important only insofar as they enable us to do important things. Assuming we have enough to eat and can afford modest housing, money is not all that important, but it still feels important. A wise friend once told me that if we seek happiness itself, we will never find it, for it is the byproduct of a meaningful life. I started my job search without thinking enough like the fisherman.

Using a variety of methodological approaches many social scientists have researched the question of how money and happiness relate. The research on that relationship is damning to the business executive's perspective and vindicates the fisherman. Most of the data gleaned in the past few decades have shown that once income exceeds approximately $12,000, more money produces virtually no increase in life satisfaction.[2] When I first saw these numbers as a college sophomore, I was shocked. I assumed it was a mistake of some sort. I spent hours looking through the research and found no problems. This revelation changed significantly the way I think about money. Once we have passed the poverty

---

2. Shankar Vedantam, "Science Confirms: You Really Can't Buy Happiness," *Washington Post,* July 3, 2006, A02.

threshold, money means very little in terms of happiness, even though it wields significant influence over our ability to buy kitchen gadgets, snazzy cars, and trendy clothes.

Later that same year, in a class on economic sociology, I learned some of the reasons why money does not make us happier once we meet a low income threshold.[3] One school[4] says that most people use wealth to buy status and that status is positional. This is the *keeping-up-with-the-Joneses* argument; people buy things to fit in with groups and measure themselves against other people. If we buy things to keep up, there will invariably be someone ahead of us, and we will always feel second best no matter how much we have. On extremely rare occasions one of us might in fact be the most wealthy person, though watching *Citizen Kane* again should remind us that this is not desirable either.

Another major school of thought argues that wealthier people tend to spend less time on happiness-related activities like family time, community, and perhaps gardening.[5] People who make a lot of money, it seems, spend a lot of time in offices doing whatever it is they do. The highest paying positions are often very stressful. It is nice to be able to leave professional responsibility behind as one leaves the office.

These two schools of thought on why happiness and money have surprisingly little connection provide useful lessons to us about how we can best spend our own money. We will feel, largely subconsciously, pressured to spend money similarly to the way our friends and co-workers spend it. If those folks spend a lot of money in ways we do not find personally meaningful, it will be difficult for us to make good decisions ourselves. It is important to find friends whose values we share to help avoid the pressure to use money for conspicuous consumption.

The second school of thought helps us think about the ways money and time relate. It is often a good choice to take a job that demands fewer hours if it means we can spend those hours with our friends, partners, community, and families. We should consider what really excites us and make sure we have time to pursue it. I make sure to make time in my life

---

3. In economics this phenomenon is called the diminishing marginal utility of money. The first dollar one earns is worth much more than the 35,000th dollar, and the 100,000th dollar has only a small fraction of the importance of the first dollar one earns. The first dollar buys the food to avoid starvation whereas the 35,000th goes toward TIVO and the 100,000th nets you a second Mojito on vacation.
4. Max Weber took this position, as did Richard Layard of the London School of Economics.
5. Alan Krueger of princeton has made arguments of this sort. *Your Money or Your Life* is a well-known book on the subject.

for cooking and eating leisurely meals with friends, for playing lots of ulti-mate Frisbee, and for working to sustain some of the wonderful commu-nities I am blessed to be a part of. The main takeaway from the practical approach to money is that we do not need much of it to be happy, and we ought to spend time doing the things that will actually make us happy.

It is not enough to think only about the ways in which money can be used to gain meaning and happiness in *our* lives. We must also consider the way our earning a living effects other people and the world at large. Several Jewish ideas have helped me think through these issues better in my life.

The biblical idea that the earth and everything on it belongs to God[6] has deep importance for the question of what is *ours* and what we should do with *our* money. From that perspective, it is not really our money at all. The property we have acquired all belongs to God. The ideas I men-tioned earlier focus on how we, as individuals, can maximize our own happiness. Those approaches are concerned with other people only inso-far as they make *us* happy. One important aspect of any Jewish approach to happiness is that in addition to being interested in *our* happiness we must also be deeply concerned with the happiness of *others*. It is not enough to go to nice restaurants, buy nice things, and enjoy our families. We must consider whether the other people with whom we share God's world can do the same. We have a slice of God's pie, so we have a respon-sibility to share that bounty and an obligation to make sure everyone has a place at the table. On the other hand, we cannot be worried only about other people, for it says in Psalms 100:2 and Deuteronomy 18:47 that we must "worship the Lord in joy." At the same time we are also famously commanded in Deuteronomy 16:20 that "Justice, justice, you [we] shall pursue!" It seems that from a Jewish perspective we have to balance our obligations to others with our own profound joy at being alive and wit-nessing the miracles of every moment.

Several years ago, while in college, I was walking down the street with a friend, and a person approached us with a request for a few dollars. I gave a dollar, and my friend also gave a dollar. As we walked away, my friend grumbled that the person we had given the money to would just use it for drugs and alcohol. "What were you going to use the money for?" I asked my friend, knowing drugs and alcohol rated high on the list. He said, "Yeah, but it's your money." It was not my money, and it was not my friend's money—it was God's money. I enter the discussion of money with

---

6. Deuteronomy 10:14.

the *kavanah,* the intention, of helping in a cosmic process of distributing resources. This moral perspective as well as the practical perspective is useful in addressing the cases in this volume.

The First Case Study

Both Ellen and Frank are in tough spots. The temptation to take lucrative jobs is great even if the companies are not. The firms they are considering working for are both behaving in deeply immoral ways, though the problems are different. The tobacco company treats its workers justly but produces a product that itself is morally problematic.[7] The clothing made by the other firm will not harm the customer but the production process is unethical; and as a result, the clothing becomes tainted as do those who profit from its production, those who make generous salaries at the company that produces it, and those who purchase the clothing, thereby perpetuating the system.

As I began the process of choosing a job after completing my BA, I primarily considered working for consulting firms and investment banks and faced a similar set of issues to those faced by Ellen and Frank. The major firms all served some clients who had major moral shortcomings. I admire my friends who can stomach the daily grind of serving clients whose behavior they cannot stand so that my friends can ultimately change the behavior of those companies and the firms who serve them. The process of becoming senior enough to have an effect in bringing justice to those workers takes years and can only be done subtly. There are some amazing people who can exist for years in the immoral firms and make a difference down the road, and perhaps Ellen and Frank are two such people.

I would have been very uncomfortable working on a case like the one McKinsey recently undertook to figure out how to cut Wal-Mart's health costs. One of their suggestions was to make all employees' jobs physically taxing so that sick and handicapped people would need to work elsewhere.[8] I am deeply thankful that I found work that I believe in as a research analyst at the Service Employees International Union (SEIU). I am hopeful that Ellen and Frank will spend many hours considering the

---

7. The Babylonian Talmud states that "it is forbidden to sell bears, lions, or anything that may injure the public" in Avodah Zara 16a. As cigarettes, when correctly used, cause significant harm to the public, it would seem they fall under this Talmudic example.

8. "Wal-mart Memo Suggests Ways to Cut Employee Benefit Costs," by Steven Greenhouse and Michael Barbaro. Published October 26, 2005. Available at www.nytimes.com/2005/10/26/business/26walmart.ready.html?ex = 1153108800&en = 8ee4046bfd78b967&ei = 5070 (accessed November 19, 2007).

changes they want to see in this world and then find work that contributes to that vision. If they can manage to avoid being corrupted by the fast-money, unscrupulous firms, I wish them luck.

If they do enter those firms, it is important for them to carefully maintain friends who have progressive values and work in helping professions; this will help Ellen and Frank avoid values-drift. It is very easy to have our values slowly change in nearly imperceptible ways. As our peers change and we have new experiences, we must be vigilant to make sure those changes are ones that take us in a direction we are happy about.

The Second Case Study

Jennifer, like so many others, was manipulated by sneaky credit card and mortgage companies.[9] The credit card company gave Jennifer more credit than she could manage. It has done this precisely because the company hopes that Jennifer will miss payments, go into debt, and thereby increase the company's profits. Leviticus 19:14 contains the prohibition against putting a stumbling block before the blind. The credit card company has put stumbling blocks before countless college students, some are blind and others not. In this case Jennifer was blind, and she was tripped. The credit card company, like any company, has an obligation to its customers to supply a product that will be mutually beneficial.

Though the credit card company has behaved immorally, that does not absolve Jennifer of the obligation to meet her bills. If she wished, she could declare bankruptcy, but this would impact her credit score. If she entered into the contract knowingly, she should have been more careful. However, if she was in fact impacted by a mental disease, she may not have been able to legitimately consent to the contract from a legal or moral standpoint. If she was unable to properly evaluate her credit-related behavior due to schizophrenia, bipolar disorder, or any other mental disease, she is not liable for the mistake. Failure to pay will likely carry practical concerns, and the decision not to pay should be taken only with extreme care and the guidance of someone familiar with the process of recovering from excessive debt.

The Third Case Study

Ira and Jackie are in the tough position of deciding how to fit children and the accompanying responsibilities into their lives. Children can fill par-

---

9. Later rabbinic thought expanded this concept to address actions that put people in situations where they are likely to commit harm, such as giving wine to a Nazarite, who has taken an oath against its consumption (Babylonian Talmud Pesachim 22b).

ents' eyes with wonder, hearts with gladness, and budgets with problems. Ira and Jackie should not cheat the government and a nanny by not paying the proper taxes and social security.

The daycare center where employees are not treated well is problematic if it does not take action to treat them better. If Ira and Jackie trust their children to the daycare center, they can work to make sure the staffers are paid well, given benefits, and allowed to unionize should they choose. These improved working conditions will likely help workers who care for their children enjoy a longer tenure at the center. This action is necessary from a moral standpoint but will also help get the best care for their children, a win–win situation. If they are not committed to ensuring the just and generous treatment of the daycare workers, then Ira and Jackie ought to make decisions that make it possible for them to care for their own children, ideally together.[10]

I sometimes get grouchy and annoyed about insignificant things when I am hungry. My mother was kind enough to help me realize this when I was a teenager, and since then, I have been able to stop to note that hunger is the primary cause of my problem rather than the issue about which I think I feel upset. Sometimes we think we are unhappy about money, and this thought hides the true cause of our concern. When we wish to buy expensive things, generally it is not because we actually need the thing nor because it will make us happier; we are responding to feelings of inadequacy, worries about status, the desire for power, or other things. It is important for us to consider what we *really* want and focus on the things that are really driving our desires rather than obsess about the money, which is only a pretext. The sooner we can get to the bottom of the attitudes and feelings that cloud our approaches to money, the happier we will be.[11] If we focus primarily on seeking money, we will not be happy. Let us instead have the wisdom to fight for justice, the courage to avoid worrying about status, the energy to organize and participate in community, and the insight to surround ourselves with wonderful people. It is in these ways that happiness will be manifest in our lives.

---

10. If they choose to take care of their children themselves, it would be wonderful for them to do it equally, avoiding the stay-at-home mom or stay-at-work dad syndrome. Sharing the work will give them each a chance to be maximally present in their children's lives and will enable them both to take active roles in the work at home and proceed with their careers.

11. It is not always the case that more expensive things do not make us any happier. For instance, I used to a go to a bar that gave shirts out to folks on their 21st birthdays that said "Life is too short for shitty beer." This too is an important lesson.

PART III

❧

CONCLUSION

Money and Morals

E VERY DAY we confront issues concerning money. What constraints are there on how we earn money and on how we spend it? How can we ensure that women and minorities receive fair compensation for their labor and attain the most prestigious (and most highly compensated) positions in society? How do we determine what constitutes fair compensation, whether for the clerk at the supermarket or the CEO of a major corporation? How much of our money should we give to those less fortunate than we, and how should we decide among the many potential recipients of our charitable giving? What moral considerations should guide the transfer of our assets to our descendents? What principles should guide the government in setting tax policy and in allocating public funds? What unique opportunities and challenges do we as Jews face in dealing with all these questions?

Throughout this volume, these questions have been addressed from a number of perspectives. Although we have not been able to consider every important moral question related to money, we hope to have prompted readers to consider some new issues and, perhaps, to reconsider familiar issues in a new light. In this essay, we wish to step back from the many particular questions listed above and consider the moral dimensions of our use of money in general. What makes the use of money such a complex and multifaceted moral issue? How does Jewish tradition offer us guidance in addressing our relationship to money? To answer these questions, we must begin by considering the many ways in which money figures in our lives.

How Money Functions in Our Lives

Money clearly pervades our lives. Whether we have it or seek it, love it or hate it, we can scarcely avoid a relationship to it. Earning and spending money are unavoidable insofar as money enables us to obtain all the goods essential to our survival—food, clothing and shelter. Investing and saving money are necessary if we wish to weather times of special needs and to secure a measure of comfort in old age when we can no longer work. The government must redistribute money in the form of taxes in order to provide all the public services and goods, from national defense to social welfare, that ensure a strong, functioning society. Bequeathing money to our children enables them to have a higher standard of living than we enjoyed. To be sure, there is much in life that money can't buy, but without money and what it buys, there would be no opportunity to enjoy all the intangible aspects of life. As the ancient Rabbis put it so succinctly, "If there is no Torah [spiritual life], there is no bread [material life], but if there is no bread, there is no Torah" (Avot 3:16).

Because money plays such an important role in our lives, it is perhaps no surprise that our relationship to it is complex and paradoxical. In many ways, money bestows power, and the more money we have, the more power we have to control the circumstances of our lives, to say nothing of the lives of others. Yet, money also has enormous power over us. In many subtle ways, our need for money and our pursuit of it can undermine our values, our sense of security and our well-being. As we explore the many ways in which money is both empowering and potentially disempowering, we will begin to appreciate why our use of money raises so many difficult ethical questions.

As we noted, the value of money derives first, and perhaps foremost, from its utility in giving us what we need to survive. But money means more to us than the means to satisfy our subsistence needs. A quick catalog of the functions and symbolic force of money makes this apparent.

Money affords us opportunities to live more fully than we otherwise could. This is not only a matter of having extra material things like sports cars and vacation homes that give us pleasure and make life more comfortable, though these are the benefits that many people have in mind when they pursue more money. The opportunity to obtain a good education (which frequently is the route to still greater earning potential as well as intellectual fulfillment), the opportunity to travel and explore various parts of the world, and the ability to partake of cultural experiences all depend on having the requisite financial resources. Money buys not only what we need to survive day to day but also what we need in order to cultivate our capacities to learn, explore, and grow.

Even more generally, money can provide us with that most precious commodity, time. We cannot create more hours in the day, of course, but by hiring people to care for our children or clean our homes, we can create more leisure time and with it the opportunity to pursue activities of our choosing. This is one of the most valuable and least appreciated aspects of having disposable income. For most people in the world, the money they have is sufficient (often, just barely so) to provide for their basic needs. For many of us fortunate enough to live in more developed and affluent societies, our surplus money can be used to purchase the services of others, providing us with a level of leisure unimaginable in other times and places.

Money can buy not only leisure but peace of mind and a certain level of security. When we have more than enough money to provide for our basic needs, we can escape from the fear of being destitute that still plagues the majority of people in the world. To be poor is to live from hand to mouth, with the constant anxiety of not having the resources to make it from one month to the next. Having sufficient money for immediate needs plus enough in reserve to provide a cushion against future needs means that we are free of this insecurity.

Having money to spare brings with it as well the power to do much for others in need. By giving our money to charitable causes of all sorts, we can ensure that those in our society born into less affluence are not deprived of basic goods and services. For those with substantial wealth and the inclination to be philanthropic, these opportunities bring the possibility of solving or helping to solve social ills such as poverty, hunger, and homelessness, as well as the possibility of making art, music, and education—including Jewish education—more broadly available. But even for those of us whose giving is on a much smaller scale, money gives us the power to make a real difference in the lives of others.

Finally, money bestows social status, especially in contemporary American society. This is reflected most obviously in the pursuit of status symbols, such as lavish homes, designer clothes, jewelry, and the like. But in more subtle ways, wealth determines social class, which in turn influences where we choose to live, with whom we are likely to associate, what positions of social prominence will be open to us, and, in general, how powerful we are in the eyes of others. Especially in a culture that has largely dispensed with the inherited status associated with royalty, money plays a major role in determining our position in society. Intellectual, political, technological, scientific, or artistic achievements are other avenues to social status, but even they depend on being funded.

None of these facts by itself is surprising, but taken together they give us a clearer picture of all the ways in which having money bestows power. Our power to obtain quality health care, to live comfortably, to have opportunities and the leisure time to enjoy them, to be free from the fear of going hungry, to provide for our children, to improve the lot of others and to obtain positions of prominence in society—all these depend, to a greater or lesser degree, on the extent of our financial security. In this light, we can begin to appreciate the cliché "Money makes the world go 'round." Not everything of value has a purchase price—some things are literally priceless—but much of what we need to flourish does.

But it is equally clear that having money, however necessary and desirable, is also dangerous. In subtle ways, money threatens to deprive us of the ability to discern our proper place in the world, what is truly important in life, and our responsibilities to others. Precisely because it is such a powerful force in our lives, money frequently overpowers all other considerations in our system of values and so makes it harder for us to live healthy, meaningful lives.

First and foremost, our awareness of the enormous value of money tends to obscure the fact that many (some would say, most) of the things we need to live fulfilling lives cannot be quantified in monetary terms at all. Putting money at the center of our lives means that we tend to commodify everything, to assume that it is available for purchase or, at least, that its value can be assessed in monetary terms. It is a truism that the best things in life are free; but in a culture of rampant consumerism and materialism, things with no price are readily dismissed as having no value.

The tendency to view things in relation to their market value also obscures other moral considerations that enter into our relationships with others. The fact that sex can be purchased from prostitutes, that votes can be purchased from politicians, or that organs can be purchased from willing donors does not, in itself, ensure that these transactions are moral. The marketplace, after all, is an amoral framework for the exchange of goods and services. With the exception of exchanges that violate the law, any buyer and any seller who can agree on a price can make a deal, irrespective of its effects on the dignity of either party or on others in society. If we judge the appropriateness of human interactions through the lens of free market principles alone, we quickly find ourselves in a world where the only value that matters is the freedom to purchase whatever our hearts desire.

There are other dangers closely connected to money, especially the temptation toward corruption. If our primary goal becomes acquiring money, soon enough it will become clear that dishonesty and fraud open many avenues to success that are foreclosed to those who are scrupulously honest. We need look no further than corporate America or the ranks of our elected officials to find ample evidence of these temptations and the frequency with which people—most of whom are already financially very secure—succumb to them. The possibility of amassing vast quantities of money in little time often proves too attractive to resist in the name of intangible goods, such as integrity and respect for the rights of others. Indeed, one of the greatest temptations associated with money is precisely to pursue it for our own benefit to the exclusion of any consideration for the rights and needs of others.

Money also has the potential to distort our views of ourselves and others. In a society that values monetary success, having less money than one would like can lead to feelings of failure and low self-esteem. By the same token, when we see others who are fabulously wealthy— corporate executives, star athletes, and entertainers—we may idolize them or judge them (positively or negatively) on the basis of their financial status alone. In all these cases, we mistake wealth, which is just one aspect of a person's identity, for the determining factor of identity. Frequently, this tendency is all the more pernicious because it is largely unconscious.

Finally, the pursuit of money, taken to its extreme, can even lead to financial ruin. The availability of easy credit, get-rich-quick schemes, and compulsive gambling are only some of the ways in which people, obsessed by a desire for more cash, make hasty and risky choices that backfire, leaving them in financial ruin. Those in desperate straits may be most susceptible to these temptations. But, as the popularity of lotteries attest, most of us at one time or another have at least contemplated ways of dramatically enhancing our wealth with a minimum of effort.

In short, when the power of money eclipses other values and goods in our lives, we worship money to the virtual exclusion of all else. When we glorify money to this extent, we subordinate our value system, our spiritual needs, our integrity, our respect for others, and (ironically) even our financial security all in the pursuit of greater wealth. When we consider the seductiveness of money and its potential to disorient our lives, we begin to appreciate that other cliché: Money is the root of all evil. Even if money is less perverse than this aphorism suggests, it certainly can distort our relationships both to ourselves and to others.

The central question we face, then, is how to establish and maintain a balanced and healthy relationship with money, one that respects its power to make our lives secure and to improve our world but that also ensures that money will not displace the other values and goods that ennoble human life.

Recent Developments That Exacerbate Moral Problems with Money

Recent developments in American society and in international commerce have made the issues surrounding the use of money more urgent than ever. Over the past few decades, the gap between the wealthiest and poorest Americans has grown dramatically. The rapid expansion of the high-technology sector of the economy, the enormous profits earned by investment banking firms, and the reduction of taxes—especially for the wealthiest segments of society—have combined to place far greater financial power in the hands of the privileged few. This, and the fact that government spending on social welfare programs has fallen as a percentage of the national budget, means that we now face new challenges if we wish to keep our society from becoming permanently divided between the haves and the have nots.

At the same time, the nations of the world are more interdependent than ever, as a result of the rapid increase in international trade, more multinational corporations, and the greater role of organizations such as the International Monetary Fund and the World Bank. Taken together, this has resulted in the outsourcing of jobs from the United States and Canada to other nations halfway around the world. But it also means that changes in economic circumstances in one place can have ripple effects in many other countries. These same developments have also created enormous new opportunities for the creation and transfer of wealth. Finally, the projected bankruptcy of the Social Security system in the United States just as the baby boomer generation begins to retire will create new challenges for people of all ages attempting to plan for their financial future.

In addition to these challenges, we live in a time when vast amounts of money are transferred electronically with a key stroke. Investment opportunities have also become increasingly varied and complex. The rise of hedge funds, derivatives, futures, and a host of other financial instruments have created a bewildering array of new ways to make money, shield it from taxes, and transfer it to others. Concomitantly, the opportunities for fraud and mismanagement of funds have also increased dramatically.

In all these ways, we live in a rapidly changing and increasingly complex economic environment. In such an environment, we are less sure than our parents or grandparents were that we will be able to provide for our own financial needs or even that we will understand the forces that are shaping our country's economic growth and stability. The opportunities to make and lose large sums of money are greater, the national economy and the international monetary system are vastly more complicated, and the social problems calling out for our charitable dollars are more numerous than ever. In short, the age-old issues of how to use money are still with us—we still need to make decisions about how to make and spend our money—but the context in which we make these decisions is arguably far more complicated now than at any time in history, making the moral questions raised in this volume even more urgent.

Jewish Guidance for the Use of Money

As the sources and essays collected in this volume attest, there is much wisdom in Jewish tradition that points in a healthy direction, even if it does not always chart a clear course through these difficult waters. Here, as in so many other cases, certain religious perspectives and sensibilities have the potential to lessen our obsession with money and to give us a moral framework within which we can discern more clearly our choices for how to use our money.

Judaism challenges many of our most fundamental assumptions about money. We almost universally assume that if we make money, it is ours. And, in one sense, this is entirely defensible. When our efforts to earn money yield results, we feel that it rightfully belongs to us. Yet, Judaism would tell us that this is to view matters from a very limited perspective. In fact, all the material prosperity that we enjoy is a gift, no matter how hard we have labored to produce it. After all, the earth and all the natural resources that sustain us are not of our making. Our bodies, which enable us to turn those resources into all the things we need in life, have capacities that we did not create and limitations that we do not control. The intellectual capacities necessary to devise new ways of earning a living—our ability to learn, to use our imagination, and to solve problems—are also innate qualities of our minds not of our own making (though, of course, we can work to enhance our natural gifts). Finally, the social conditions needed to create wealth, such as political stability and the opportunity for commercial trade, are largely beyond our personal control. If we are fortunate to live in a society that embraces democratic values and free enterprise, we are far more likely to accumulate money than would otherwise be the case. For all these reasons, the money we earn is only very partially the fruit of our own efforts, and so Judaism teaches us to be grateful to God for our prosperity and not to take undue credit for our material success. The Torah puts this very directly and succinctly: "Beware lest your heart grow haughty and you forget the Lord your God . . . and you say to yourselves, 'My own power and the might of my own hand have won this wealth for me.' Remember that it is the Lord your God who gives you the power to get wealth, in fulfillment of the covenant that He made on oath with your fathers" (Deuteronomy 8:14,17–18).

This view that our wealth is not fully our own finds expression in many of Judaism's other teachings about the ways in which we should, and should not, use our money. Perhaps most striking, the Torah requires us to provide for the poor and the marginalized in society whenever we reap the benefits of our labor. The corner of the field that may not be harvested, the stalks that are dropped, the sheaf that is forgotten—at every stage of the harvesting process, we are commanded to share our wealth with those less fortunate (Leviticus 19:9–10; Deuteronomy 24:19–21). These rules were clearly designed not only to remind farmers that the land and its produce are not theirs alone but also to reinforce the principle that everyone in society must share in the collective good fortune of others. Our responsibility to care for one another is emphasized precisely at the point when the temptation to selfishness and feelings of entitlement are likely to be strongest.

The Torah places a curb not only on our tendency toward selfishness but also on our power to use our financial power to oppress others. The biblical laws that forbid charging usurious interest and charging interest to other members of one's own community altogether (Exodus 22:24; Leviticus 25:35–37; Deuteronomy 23:20–21) restrict the power of those with money to take unfair advantage of those who need it. Moreover, the biblical rule requiring that all debts be cancelled every seventh year ensures that creditors cannot use their financial advantage to create a permanent class of debtors (Deuteronomy 15:1–3). It is interesting that when this rule was circumvented in rabbinic times (through a legal device that permitted courts to collect loans after the seventh year on behalf of creditors), it was out of consideration for the debtors, not the creditors (Mishnah Shebiit 10:3). In the last few years of the sabbatical cycle, lenders would be understandably reluctant to loan money, making it very difficult for the poor to borrow what they needed. Recognizing this problem, the Rabbis attempted to ensure that the poor did not become destitute and those with money to lend would still be willing to extend credit to those in need. These rules plainly restrict the freedom of the marketplace in ways that work to the advantage of the economically underprivileged and curb the power of the wealthy. The Torah's point could not be clearer: The power of those with money must be restricted in order to ensure that those on the bottom of the economic ladder are not permanently disenfranchised or harmed.

But the tradition addresses more than the proper use of our wealth; our attitude toward money, however much we may have, is also a matter of concern. Jewish teachers over the centuries have cautioned against allowing the value of money to eclipse other values in life. When the Sages ask, "Who is rich?" the answer is not "the person with the highest salary," or "the one who has a monopoly in the marketplace," or "the one who has the greatest net worth." Instead, we are told that it is "those who are satisfied with their share" who are truly richest (Avot 4:1). The goal is not to amass more wealth but to cultivate more serenity with the material success one has, to focus not on the size of one's checkbook but on the ability to put one's financial resources in proper perspective. It is worth noting here that the poor are not exalted and the goal is not to renounce material possessions. "Blessed are you poor, for yours is the kingdom of God" (Luke 6:20) is not a Jewish teaching, for the Rabbis recognized the importance of having the financial means to serve God and to sustain the community. Still, what matters ultimately is not how much we have but our ability to ensure that acquiring money remains a means to an end, rather than an end in itself.

Traditional Jewish sources will not provide us with detailed or easy answers to contemporary moral problems with money, especially in light of the recent developments noted above that make those problems even more difficult. Certainly it would be unrealistic to imagine that rules reflecting the use of money in the agrarian society of biblical times or the slightly more complicated mercantile society of rabbinic times would be well suited to the era of Internet banking and international commerce. But it is equally clear that the need for values to guide our decisions about money remains unchanged; indeed, our need for a set of core values to keep the power of money from overpowering us is greater than ever.

Among these values, we wish to highlight a few that we find within Jewish tradition and that we believe will remain key components in any Jewish ethic of money in the years ahead.

Honesty: Earning money honestly, without misrepresentation or fraud, and compensating those who work for us fairly, without taking advantage of their vulnerabilities, are essential to creating and preserving trust between people. Any system in which these are not core values will quickly degenerate into a free-for-all in which the most powerful exploit and seriously harm those most at risk.

Humility: Recognizing that our money is the product of many hands besides our own and of forces beyond our control will tend to curb our tendency to self-satisfaction and self-aggrandizement. We will use our money best if we approach each decision with a sense of gratitude, rather than of entitlement.

Generosity: Our lives and our destinies are bound up with others in our society and, increasingly, around the world. Our willingness to share liberally of what we have with those less fortunate is essential to securing the common good and protecting the human dignity of every person.

Extrinsic Value of Money: Money must not be seen as intrinsically valuable, something to be sought for its own sake. Rather, money is valuable solely for the ways in which it enables us to survive, and then to live more fully. If we keep this perspective at the forefront of our minds, we will be less susceptible to the ways in which money can come to "own" us, and we will more likely establish a healthy relationship to money—one in which moral values define our use of money, rather than the reverse.

Money, or its functional equivalent, will be with us for the foreseeable future. The reasons why we need it and the questions about how to spend it will remain essentially unchanged, even if the opportunities for earning it and the temptations for abusing it grow exponentially. Without a set of values to guide us, money itself will become the guide, the end, and the standard by which we judge means to that end. But because money itself is value free, this can only mean surrendering all moral considerations in the pursuit of greater amounts of money and greater freedom in using it. With the help of Jewish values such as the ones we have outlined here, however, we have the ability to ensure that one of the most powerful tools for human flourishing continues to be harnessed for good.

Glossary

adamah Ground.

brit milah Circumcision. Traditionally performed on a baby boy on the eighth day after his birth. See Genesis 17.

chai Life.

challah/challot The special twisted egg bread traditionally made for the Sabbath and other Jewish holidays.

dina d'malkhuta dina "The law of the land is the law." The talmudic rule that Jews are subject to the legal authority of the non-Jewish societies in which they live (Babylonian Talmud Nedarim 28a; Gittin 10b; Bava Kamma 113a; Bava Batra 54b–55a)

dover emet bilvavo Lit., "speaking honestly in one's heart." Being honest with oneself.

Ehyeh asher ehyeh "I Am-Was-Will Be Who/What I Am-Was-Will Be." The explanation God offers to Moses of God's name, meant to emphasize the impenetrable mystery of God's nature or perhaps God's transcending of time or causality. See Exodus 3:14.

goy/goyim Lit., "nation(s), non-Jew(s)." Sometimes used with derogatory connotations.

halakhah Jewish Law.

Havdalah Lit. "separation." The ceremony on Saturday night that separates the Sabbath from the rest of the week.

hesed Lit., "lovingkindness." One of the qualities of God and one of the virtues that Jews aspire to emulate.

hevruta Lit., "partner." In traditional Jewish text study, students work in pairs.

hiddur mitzvah Lit., "beautification of a commandment." A traditional concept that a biblical commandment should be performed in a way that is aesthetically pleasing and uplifting rather than perfunctory.

kashrut Kosher, the dietary rules prescribed by the Torah and expanded by the Rabbis that are observed by traditional Jews. See Leviticus 11 and Deuteronomy 14 for some of these laws.

kavanah Intention, a concept with wide-ranging application in Jewish law, especially in relation to the proper performance of a ritual act or in matters of liability in civil and criminal affairs.

kavod Honor, frequently used in connection with the honor due one's parents, or more generally of honoring God's creatures.

kiddush Lit., "sanctification." The prayer said over a cup of wine at the beginning of Sabbath and holiday meals.

klei kodesh Holy instruments (or holy articles). Sometimes used metaphorically for rabbis, cantors, and Jewish educators.

koach Force, power.

kol Yisrael arevim ze le ze "All Jews are responsible for one another" (Babylonian Talmud Shevuot 39a). This talmudic phrase reflects the strong traditional values of Jews' interdependence and their collective responsibility.

kup Lit., "head" (Yiddish). Used figuratively as well as literally, as in "He has a good *kup* for Talmud study."

lifnim meshurat hadin Supererogation. Doing more than the law requires (or pressing one's legal claims less than the law permits).

lo tishkach "Never forget."

malach/malachim Messenger (whether human or divine).

mechitzah A partition separating men and women in Orthodox synagogues.

mensch/menschlikhkeit Lit. "man/humanity" (Yiddish). Refers to the popular traditional concept of human decency; one who is morally honorable and sensitive to the needs of others is said to be a "mensch."

middat ha-din The attribute of strict justice; one of God's two main attributes in relationship with humankind.

middat ha-rachamim The attribute of mercy or compassion; one of God's two main attributes.

mikveh Ritual bath, used by women for purification after the conclusion of their menstrual periods before reestablishing sexual relations with their husbands, also as part of the ritual for conversation to Judaism and in other instances of ritual or spiritual purification. See Leviticus 15 and Numbers 19.

minyan Lit., "quorum." The 10 adults (traditionally, 10 adult men) required to constitute a quorum for purposes of public prayer.

mi sheberakh A prayer for healing named for the first two words of the traditional Hebrew text, "May the one who blessed . . . [our ancestors . . . bless those who are ill . . .]."

mishkan Lit., "dwelling place." The name of the ancient Tabernacle that the Israelites carried with them during their wanderings in the desert. The Tabernacle, and later the permanent Temple in Jerusalem, were understood as the place where God's presence dwelled on earth.

Mishnah Lit. "teaching." The name of the Hebrew law code written in Palestine circa 200 c.e., traditionally ascribed to Rabbi Judah the Prince. The Mishnah greatly expands upon biblical law and later becomes the foundation of the Talmud.

mitzvah/mitzvot "Commandment(s)." One of the Torah's laws. According to tradition, there were 613 divinely ordained mitzvot in the Torah.

mohel Ritual circumcisor.

nigun Lit, "melody." One of the haunting wordless melodies sung by Hasidic Jews.

ona'ah Lit. "coercion." Unfair exploitation through overcharging.

parashah Torah portion, the set reading from the Pentateuch for a given Sabbath or holiday, usually encompassing several chapters.

Rosh Hodesh The new moon, which marks the beginning of the new month in the Hebrew calendar. Some contemporary Jewish women have created ceremonies to celebrate Rosh Hodesh.

ruach Spirit.

Selichot Petitions for forgiveness.

shtetl One of the small, predominantly Jewish villages of eastern Europe from which many Jews emigrated to America or Israel.

shtetl bubbes Jewish grandmothers.

Shulchan Arukh "The set table." The name of the classic code of Jewish law composed by Rabbi Joseph Caro (1488–1575) and completed in 1565.

teshuvah "An answer." A rabbinic ruling in response to a question in Jewish law. Also, lit., "turning" or "response," repentance, one of the key moral aspects of Jewish life.

tikkun olam Lit., "repair of the world." The idea, central to Jewish tradition, that it is the task of humankind to complete the process of creation that God began. The concept takes on special cosmological significance in the work of the Kabbalists, or Jewish mystics.

tikvah Hope.

tokhehah Obligation to reprove (those who transgress). See Leviticus 19:17.

tzeniut Lit., "modesty." Used most often in connection with the traditional value that women should dress in a way that is not revealing or sexually provocative.

yetzer ha-ra Lit., "evil inclination." That aspect of human nature that prompts us to sin.

zachor Remember.

Suggestions for Further Reading
General Sources on Jewish Ethics

Abramowitz, Yosef I., and Susan Silverman. *Jewish Family & Life: Traditions, Holidays, and Values for Today's Parents and Children*. New York: Golden Books, 1997.

Agus, Jacob B. *The Vision and the Way: An Interpretation of Jewish Ethics*. New York: Frederick Ungar Publishing, 1966.

Alpert, Rebecca T., and Jacob J. Staub. *Exploring Judaism: A Reconstructionist Approach*. Expanded and Updated. Jenkintown, Pa.: Jewish Reconstructionist Federation, 2000.

Amsel, Nachum. *The Jewish Encyclopedia of Moral and Ethical Issues*. Northvale, N.J.: Jason Aronson, 1994.

Birnbaum, Philip. *Encyclopedia of Jewish Concepts*. New York: Hebrew Publishing Company, 1964, 1995.

Borowitz, Eugene B. *Exploring Jewish Ethics: Papers on Covenant Responsibility*. Detroit, Mich.: Wayne State University Press, 1990.

_____, ed. *Reform Jewish Ethics and the Halakhah*. West Orange, N.J.: Behrman House, 1994.

Borowitz, Eugene B., and Frances Weinman Schwartz. *The Jewish Moral Virtues*. Philadelphia: The Jewish Publication Society, 1999.

Breslauer, S. Daniel. *A New Jewish Ethics*. New York & Toronto: Edwin Mellon Press, 1983.

Cohen, Jeffery. *Dear Chief Rabbi: From the Correspondence of Chief Rabbi Immanuel Jakobovits on Matters of Jewish Law, Ethics, and Contemporary Issues, 1980–1990*. Hoboken, N.J.: Ktav, 1995.

Cohn, Haim. *Human Rights in Jewish Law*. New York: Ktav (Institute of Jewish Affairs, London), 1984.

Dan, Joseph. *Jewish Mysticism and Jewish Ethics*. Philadelphia: The Jewish Publication Society, 1986.

Dorff, Elliot N. "The Ethics of Judaism. " In *The Blackwell Companion to Judaism,* ed. by Jacob Neusner and Alan J. Avery-Peck, 373–392. Oxford: Blackwell Publishers, 2000.

_____. *Love Your Neighbor and Yourself: A Jewish Approach to Modern Personal Ethics*. Philadelphia: The Jewish Publication Society, 2003.

_____. *Matters of Life and Death: A Jewish Approach to Modern Medical Ethics*. Philadelphia: The Jewish Publication Society, 1998.

_____. *To Do the Right and the Good: A Jewish Approach to Modern Personal Ethics*. Philadelphia: The Jewish Publication Society, 2002.

_____. *The Way into Tikkun Olam (Fixing the World)*. Woodstock, Vt.: Jewish Lights, 2005.

Dorff, Elliot N., and Louis E. Newman, eds. *Contemporary Jewish Ethics and Morality: A Reader*. New York: Oxford University Press, 1995.

Dorff, Elliot N., and Arthur Rosett. *A Living Tree: The Roots and Growth of Jewish Law*. Albany: State University of New York Press, 1988.

Dresner, Samuel H., and Byron L. Sherwin. *Judaism: The Way of Sanctification*. New York: United Synagogue of America, 1978.

Fox, Marvin, ed. *Modern Jewish Ethics: Theory and Practice*. Columbus: Ohio State University Press, 1975.

Freund, Richard A. *Understanding Jewish Ethics*. 2 vols. Lewiston, N.Y.: Edwin Mellon Press, 1990 (vol. 1) and 1993 (vol. 2).

Goldman, Alex J. *Judaism Confronts Contemporary Issues*. New York: Shengold Publishers, 1978.

Goldstein, Niles E., and Steven S. Mason. *Judaism and Spiritual Ethics*. New York: Union of American Hebrew Congregations Press, 1996.

Goodman, Lenn E. *Judaism, Human Rights, and Human Values*. New York : Oxford University Press, 1998.

Gordis, Robert. *The Dynamics of Judaism: A Study in Jewish Law*. Bloomington: Indiana University Press, 1990.

_____. *Judaic Ethics for a Lawless World*. New York: Jewish Theological Seminary of America, 1986.

Jacobs, Louis. *Jewish Personal and Social Ethics*. West Orange, N.J.: Behrman House, 1990.

Kadushin, Max. *Worship and Ethics: A Study in Rabbinic Judaism*. Evanston, Ill.: Northwestern University Press, 1964.

Kaplan, Mordecai M. *The Future of the American Jew*. New York: Reconstructionist Press, 1948, 1967.

Kellner, Menachem Marc, ed. *Contemporary Jewish Ethics*. New York: Sanhedrin Press, 1978.

Klagsbrun, Francine. *Voices of Wisdom: Jewish Ideas and Ethics for Everyday Living*. New York: Pantheon Books, 1980. (Reprinted, Philadelphia: The Jewish Publication Society.)

Malsin, Simeon J., ed. *Gates of Mitzvah—Shaarei Mitzvah*. New York: Central Conference of American Rabbis Press, 1986.

Suggestions for Further Reading

Meir, Asher. *The Jewish Ethicist: Everyday Ethics for Business and Life.* Jersey City, N.J.: Ktav and Business Ethics Center of Jerusalem, 2005.

Newman, Louis E. *An Introduction to Jewish Ethics.* Upper Saddle River, N.J.: Pearson Prentice Hall, 2005.

_____. *Past Imperatives: Studies in the History and Theory of Jewish Ethics.* Albany: State University of New York Press, 1998.

Novak, David. *Jewish Social Ethics.* New York : Oxford University Press, 1992.

Olitzky, Kerry M., and Rachel T. Sabath. *Striving toward Virtue: A Contemporary Guide for Jewish Ethical Behavior.* Hoboken, N.J.: Ktav, 1996.

Sacks, Jonathan. *To Heal a Fractured World: The Ethics of Responsibility.* New York: Schocken Books, 2005.

Schwarz, Sidney. *Judaism and Justice: The Jewish Passion to Repair the World.* Woodstock, Vt.: Jewish Lights, 2006.

Shatz, David, Chaim I. Waxman, and Nathan J. Diament, eds. *Tikkun Olam: Social Responsibility in Jewish Thought and Law.* Northvale, N.J.: Jason Aronson, 1997.

Sherwin, Byron L. *Jewish Ethics for the Twenty-First Century: Living in the Image of God.* Syracuse, N.Y.: Syracuse University Press, 2000.

Sherwin, Byron L., and Seymour J. Cohen. *Creating An Ethical Jewish Life: A Practical Introduction to Classic Teachings on How to Be a Jew.* Woodstock, Vt.: Jewish Lights, 2001.

_____. *How to Be a Jew: Ethical Teachings of Judaism.* Northvale, N.J.: Jason Aronson, 1992.

Siegel, Richard, Michael Strassfield, and Sharon Strassfield, eds. *The Jewish Catalogue.* Philadelphia: The Jewish Publication Society of America, 1973.

Stone, Ira. *A Responsible Life: The Spiritual Path of Mussar.* New York: Aviv Press and the Rabbinical Assembly, 2006.

Telushkin, Joseph. *A Code of Jewish Ethics.* Vol. 1: *You Shall Be Holy.* New York: Bell Tower, 2006.

_____. *Jewish Wisdom: Ethical, Spiritual, and Historical Lessons from the Great Works and Thinkers.* New York: William Morrow, 1994.

Vorspan, Albert, and David Saperstein. *Tough Choices: Jewish Perspectives on Social Justice.* New York: Union of American Hebrew Congregations Press, 1992.

Washofsky, Mark. *Jewish Living: A Guide to Contemporary Reform Practice.* New York: Union of American Hebrew Congregations, 2001.

Wurzburger, Walter S. *Ethics of Responsibility: Pluralistic Approaches to Covenantal Ethics.* Philadelphia: The Jewish Publication Society, 1994.

Jewish Sources on Ethical Issues Concerning Money

Arkin, Marcus. *Aspects of Jewish Economic History*. Philadelphia: The Jewish Publication Society of America, 1975.

Baron, Salo. "The Economic Views of Maimonides." In *Ancient and Medieval Jewish History,* ed. Leon A. Feldman, 149–236. New Brunswick, N.J.: Rutgers University Press, 1972.

Benstein, Jeremy. "Advertising and the Tenth Commandment." *The Jerusalem Report*, August 13, 2001.

Bick, Ezra. "Payment of Income Taxes: Halachic Guidelines." In *Contemporary Jewish Ethics,* ed. Marc Kellner, 344–346. New York: Sanhedrin Press, 1978.

Bleich, J. David. "Business and Commerce." In *Contemporary Halakhic Problems* (II: 120–128). New York: Ktav Publishing House and Yeshiva University Press, 1983.

_____. "Heter Iska. [Loans]." In *Contemporary Halakhic Problems* (II: 376–384). New York: Ktav Publishing House and Yeshiva University Press, 1983.

_____. "Organized Labor." In *Contemporary Halakhic Problems* (I: 186–189). New York: Ktav Publishing House and Yeshiva University Press, 1977.

_____. "Physicians' Fees." In *Contemporary Halakhic Problems* (II: 68–74). New York: Ktav Publishing House and Yeshiva University Press, 1983.

_____. "Physicians' Strikes." In *Contemporary Halakhic Problems* (III:18–25). New York: Ktav Publishing House and Yeshiva University Press, 1989.

_____. "Rabbinic Contracts." In *Contemporary Halakhic Problems* (I: 71–73). New York: Ktav Publishing House and Yeshiva University Press, 1977.

_____. "Teachers' Unions." In *Contemporary Halakhic Problems* (II:111–113). New York: Ktav Publishing House and Yeshiva University Press, 1983.

Champagne, Jess. "Jewish Activism and United Students against Sweatshops." Available at www.socialaction.com/issues/human_civil/labor/sweatshops.shtml (accessed December 11, 2006).

Cohen, Gerson. "The Unwritten Law of Business in the Talmud." Chap. 21 in *Jewish History and Destiny.* New York: Jewish Theological Seminary of America, 1997.

Cohen, Seymour. "Judaism and the Worlds of Business and Labor." *Proceedings of the Rabbinical Assembly* 25 (1961): 17–44.

Dorff, Elliot N. *To Do the Right and the Good: A Jewish Approach to Modern Social Ethics*. Philadelphia: The Jewish Publication Society, 2002.

_____. *The Way into Tikkun Olam (Fixing the World)*. Woodstock, Vt.: Jewish Lights, 2005.

Dosick, Wayne. *The Business Bible: Ten Commandments for Creating an Ethical Workplace.* New York: William Morrow, 1993.

Feigelson, Mimi, and Rabbi Leon Wiener-Dow. "Investigating Tzedakah Requests: A Talmudic Inquiry." In *Seeing Need, Envisioning Change: A Ta Shma Conversation Piece in Memory of Charles Schusterman,* ed. Leon Wiener-Dow pp. 5–6 and 13–14. Ta Shma: Pluralistic Jewish Learning, 2001.

Gross, Nachum, ed. *Economic History of the Jews.* New York: Schocken, 1975.

Holtz, Barry W. "A World of Justice." Chap. 7 in *Finding Our Way: Jewish Texts and the Lives We Live Today.* New York: Schocken, 1990.

Herman, Stewart W., ed. with Arthur Gross Schaefer. *Spiritual Goods: Faith Traditions and the Practice of Business.* Charlottesville, Va.: Philosophy Documentation Center, 2001.

Herring, Basil. "Truth and Deception in the Marketplace." Chap. 6 in *Jewish Ethics and Halakhah for Our Time,* vol. 2. Hoboken, N.J.: Ktav and New York: Yeshiva University Press, 1989.

Jung, Leo. "The Ethics of Business." In *Contemporary Jewish Ethics,* ed. Menachem Marc Kellner, 332–343. New York: Sanhedrin Press, 1978.

Jung, Leo, and Aaron Levine. *Business Ethics in Jewish Law.* New York: Hebrew Publishing, 1987.

Kirschenbaum, Aaron. *Equity in Jewish Law.* 2 vols. Hoboken, N.J.: Ktav and New York: Yeshiva University Press, 1991.

Klein, Isaac. *Responsa and Halakhic Studies.* 1975; Jerusalem: The Institute of Applied Halakhah of the Schechter Institute of Jewish Studies, 2005.

Lappin, Daniel. *Thou Shalt Prosper.* Hoboken, N.J.: John Wiley & Sons, 2002.

Levine, Aaron. *Case Studies in Jewish Business Ethics.* Hoboken, N.J.: Ktav and New York: Yeshiva University Press, 1999.

_____. *Economics and Jewish Law.* Hoboken, N.J.: Ktav Publishing House and New York: Yeshiva University Press, 1987.

_____. *Economic Public Policy and Jewish Law.* Hoboken, N.J.: Ktav and New York: Yeshiva University Press, 1993.

_____. *Free Enterprise and Jewish Law: Aspects of Jewish Business Ethics.* New York: Ktav and Yeshiva University Press, 1980.

_____. *Moral Issues of the Marketplace in Jewish Law.* Brooklyn, N.Y.: Yashar Books, 2005.

_____ and Moses L Pava, eds. *Jewish Business Ethics: The Firm and Its Stakeholders.* Northvale, N.J.: Jason Aronson, 1999.

Loewenberg, Frank. *From Charity to Social Justice: The Emergence of Communal Institutions for the Support of the Poor in Ancient Judaism.* New Brunswick, N.J.: Transaction Publishers, 2001.

Meir, Asher. *The Jewish Ethicist: Everyday Ethics for Business and Life.* Jersey City, N.J.: Ktav and Jerusalem, Israel: Business Ethics Center of Jerusalem, 2005.

Neusner, Jacob. *The Economics of the Mishnah.* Chicago: University of Chicago Press, 1990.

Perry, Grant. "The 'Good Jew' Who Went to Jail." *Reform Judaism Magazine* 31:2 (winter 2002): 26.

Pomerance, Rachel. "Engaging the Next Generation: Rich Young Jews Talk about Money." Available at jta.org/page_view_story.asp?intarticleid = 15219&int categoryid = 4 (accessed December 2, 2006).

Rakover, Nahum. *Ethics in the Market Place: A Jewish Perspective.* Jerusalem: The Library of Jewish Law, 2000.

_____. "Unjust Enrichment." In *Essential Papers on the Talmud,* ed. Michael Chernick, 331–356. New York: New York University Press, 1994.

Siegel, Danny. *Angels: Essays.* Spring Valley, N.Y.: Town House Press, 1980.

Siegel, Seymour. "A Jewish View of Economic Justice." In *Contemporary Jewish Ethics and Morality: A Reader,* ed. Elliot Dorff and Louis Newman, 336–343. Oxford: Oxford University Press, 1995.

———. *Good People.* Pittsboro, N.C.: Town House Press, 1995.

_____. *Gym Shoes and Irises: Personalized Tzedakah.* Spring Valley, N.Y.: Town House Press, 1982.

———. *Mitzvahs.* Pittsboro, N.C.: Town House Press, 1990.

_____. *Munbaz II and Other Mitzvah Heroes.* Spring Valley, N.Y.: Town House Press, 1988.

Spitzer, Jeffery. "Preventing dependency." Available at www.myjewishlearning .com/daily_life/Tzedakah/TO_Tzedakah_Requirements/Preventing_Dependency. htm (accessed December 2, 2006).

Tamari, Meir. *The Challenge of Wealth: A Jewish Perspective on Earning and Spending Money.* Northvale, N.J.: Jason Aronson, 1995.

_____. *In the Marketplace: Jewish Business Ethics.* Southfield, Mich.: Targum Press, 1991.

_____. *With All Your Possessions: Jewish Ethics and Economic Life.* Northvale: N.J.: Jason Aronson, 1998.

Suggestions for Further Reading

Teutsch, David. *A Guide to Jewish Practice: Organizational, Business, and Commercial Ethics*. Wyncote, Pa.: Reconstructionist Rabbinical College, 2007.

_____. *A Guide to Jewish Practice: Tzedaka*. Wyncote, Pa.: Reconstructionist Rabbinical College, 2005.

_____. "Values Decision Making." *Reconstructionist* 65:2 (spring 2001): 22–28.

Tucker, Gordon. "Jewish Sources on Business Practices." *Proceedings of the Rabbinical Assembly* 49 (1989): 258–269.

Wagschal, S. *Torah Guide to Money Matters for Home, Business, and Everyday Life*. Nanuet & Jerusalem: Feldheim Publishers, 1996.

Waskow, Arthur. *Down-to-Earth Judaism: Food, Money, Sex, and the Rest of Life*. New York: W. Morrow, 1995.

Wilson, Rodney. *Economics, Ethics, and Religion: Jewish, Christian and Muslim Economic Thought*. New York: New York University Press, 1997.

Zinbarg, Edward. *Faith, Morals and Money: What the World's Religions Tell Us about Ethics in the Marketplace*. New York: Continuum, 2001.

Zipperstein, Edward. *Business Ethics in Jewish Law*. New York: Ktav, 1983.

Editors and Contributors

Editors

Elliot N. Dorff, rabbi (Jewish Theological Seminary), Ph.D. (Columbia University), is rector and Sol and Anne Dorff Distinguished Professor of Philosophy at the American Jewish University (formerly the University of Judaism) in Los Angeles. Among his 14 books are 3 award-winning Jewish Publication Society books on Jewish ethics. He and Louis Newman are co-editors of *Contemporary Jewish Ethics and Morality* (Oxford, 1995) and *Contemporary Jewish Theology* (Oxford, 1999). Since 1984 Dorff has served on the Rabbinical Assembly's Committee on Jewish Law and Standards, currently as its chair. He also has served on several federal government advisory commissions dealing with the ethics of health care, sexual responsibility, and research on human subjects; and he currently is a member of California's Ethics Committee on embryonic stem cell research.

Louis E. Newman, Ph.D. (Brown University), is the John M. and Elizabeth W. Musser Professor of Religious Studies and director of Judaic studies at Carleton College. He is the author of *Past Imperatives: Studies in the History and Theory of Jewish Ethics* (1998) and *An Introduction to Jewish Ethics* (2005), as well as co-editor with Elliot Dorff of two anthologies (see above). He is currently working on a book on Jewish views of repentance.

Contributors

Sara Berman is the parenting columnist for *The New York Sun*. She is a frequent guest on Fox News Network and *CBS News This Morning*. She lives in New York City with her husband and four children.

Michael B. Dorff is the associate dean for research and a professor of law at Southwestern Law School in Los Angeles, where he teaches contracts, business associations, and corporate mergers and acquisitions. He has written law review articles on executive compensation in public corporations as well as articles on the philosophy of law and economics and the theory of contract law. A graduate of Harvard College and Harvard Law School, he has also taught at Rutgers Law School in Camden, New Jersey.

Solomon J. Freedman is an attorney who has been in practice for over fifty-five years specializing in trusts and estates and real property. As an attorney, he has represented families in multigenerational transfers of business and wealth. By avocation, for over forty years he has been a student of the Talmud and Scripture. It is his conviction that by applying talmudic logic and quoting known scriptural passages and Yiddish witticisms to many of his clients, he has diffused seemingly irreconcilable differences between parents and children and among business partners and has helped them find their paths toward settlement, restoring the concern, respect, and even love that they had for each other.

Sally Gottesman is a consultant to not-for-profit organizations in New York City and the chair of Moving Traditions.

Jill Jacobs is the director of education for the Jewish Funds for Justice, a national public foundation dedicated to mobilizing the resources of American Jews to combat the root causes of domestic social and economic injustice. She holds rabbinic ordination and an M.A. in Talmud from the Jewish Theological Seminary as well as an M.S. in urban affairs from Hunter College.

Jonathan Lopatin, a retired partner at Goldman, Sachs & Co., is currently a graduate student at the Jewish Theological Seminary and a board member of a number of Jewish philanthropies.

Michael Masch is the secretary of budget and administration for the state of Pennsylvania. Before his appointment as secretary of the budget, he served as vice president for budget and management analysis at the University of Pennsylvania, where he continues to teach. He majored in urban studies as an undergraduate at Temple University and received his masters degree in government administration from the University of Pennsylvania.

Susan Schwartzman is director of the Peninsula Jewish Community Teen Foundation and the regional coordinator of Youth Philanthropy for the Jewish Community Endowment Fund of the Jewish Community Federation of San Francisco, Marin, and Sonoma Counties. She also has an education consulting practice, focusing on standards of excellence in curriculum, teaching practices, and the integration of Jewish values into the secular curriculum. She holds a B.A. from the University of California at Davis in psychology and drama, a secondary teaching credential, and an M.A. in education from Stanford University.

Fridelle Zaiman Spiegel is the author of *Women's Wages, Women's Worth: Politics, Religion, and Equity* (Continuum, 1994). She holds doctorates in both religion and psychoanalysis and has served on the faculties of the department of history at the University of California at Los Angeles (UCLA) and the New Center for Psychoanalysis. A psychoanalyst in private practice, she was the founding director of the Israel-Diaspora program at UCLA. She is currently at work on a book exploring psychoanalytic interpretations of contemporary Jewish issues.

Alana Suskin received her rabbinic ordination and masters of rabbinic studies from the University of Judaism's Ziegler School of Rabbinic Studies. She holds an M.A. in philosophy, a graduate certificate in women's studies from the University of Maryland, and B.A. degrees in both philosophy and Russian. She is a popular speaker on social justice/transformation and on feminism and Judaism. Her poetry, essays, and articles have been widely published.

David A. Teutsch, rabbi (Hebrew Union College–Jewish Institute of Religion, New York), Ph.D. (Wharton School, University of Pennsylvania), is the Wiener Professor of Contemporary Jewish Civilization and director of the Levin-Lieber Program in Jewish ethics at the Reconstructionist Rabbinical College (RRC) in Philadelphia. A past president of RRC and the Academic Coalition of Jewish Bioethics and current president of the Society of Jewish Ethics, he is the author or editor of a dozen books and is currently at work on a comprehensive, values-based guide to Jewish practice.

Zachary Teutsch is the coordinator of Investment Education for the American Federation of State, County, and Municipal Workers (AFSCME) AFL-CIO. In addition to being an organizer of Tikkun Leil Shabbat, he serves on the boards of the Jewish Reconstructionist Federation and Moishe House Boston: Kavod Jewish Social Justice House.

Index